Cross Stitch Chart & Pattern Sketchbook

×××

Four Sizes of Stitch Count Graphs
On 10 Square Grid
With Fill In Floss Charts

Hoop & Thread Needlework Design

CONTENTS

1   100 x 120 Stitch Count 10-Square Graph Grids   1

2   80 x 100 Stitch Count 10-Square Graph Grids   Pg 43

3   60 x 80 Stitch Count 10-Square Graph Grids   Pg 85

4   40 x 60 Stitch Count 10-Square Graph Grids   Pg 127

100 X 120
Stitch Count

10-Square Graph Grids

Floss Chart

STRAND	TYPE	NUMBER	COLOR	ALTERNATE

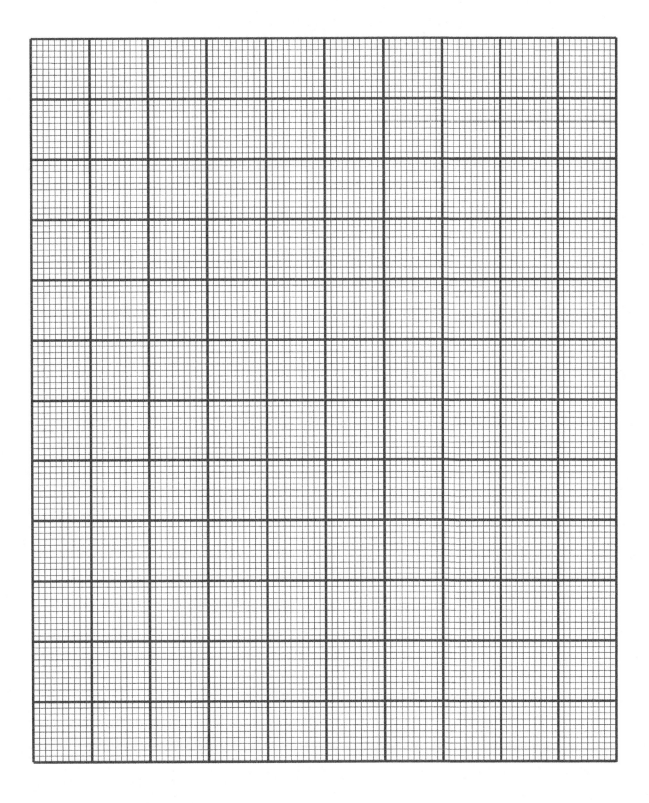

Floss Chart

STRAND	TYPE	NUMBER	COLOR	ALTERNATE

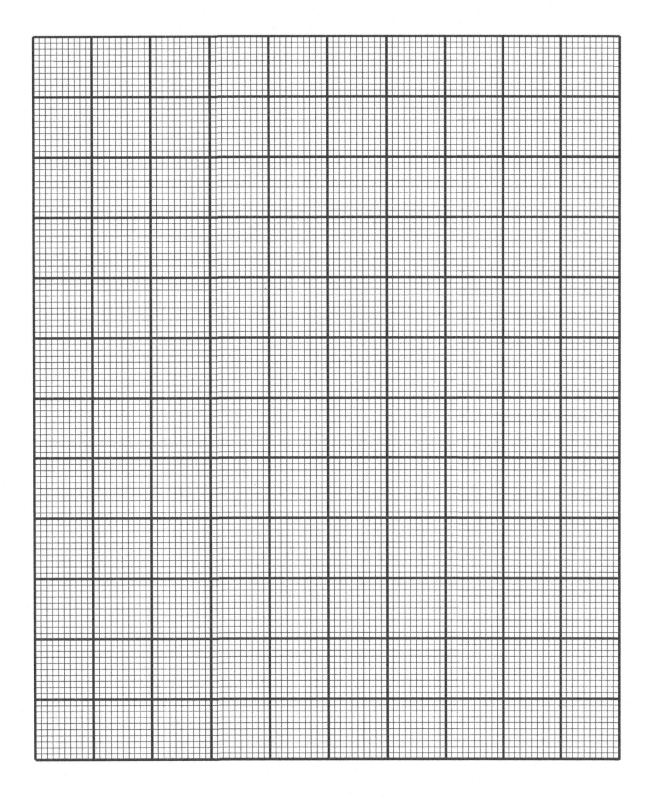

Floss Chart

	STRAND	TYPE	NUMBER	COLOR	ALTERNATE
•					
○					
▪					
✚					
△					
◆					
=					
✖					
★					
⊙					
▣					
#					
▼					
☐					
☐					
▽					
→					
☽					

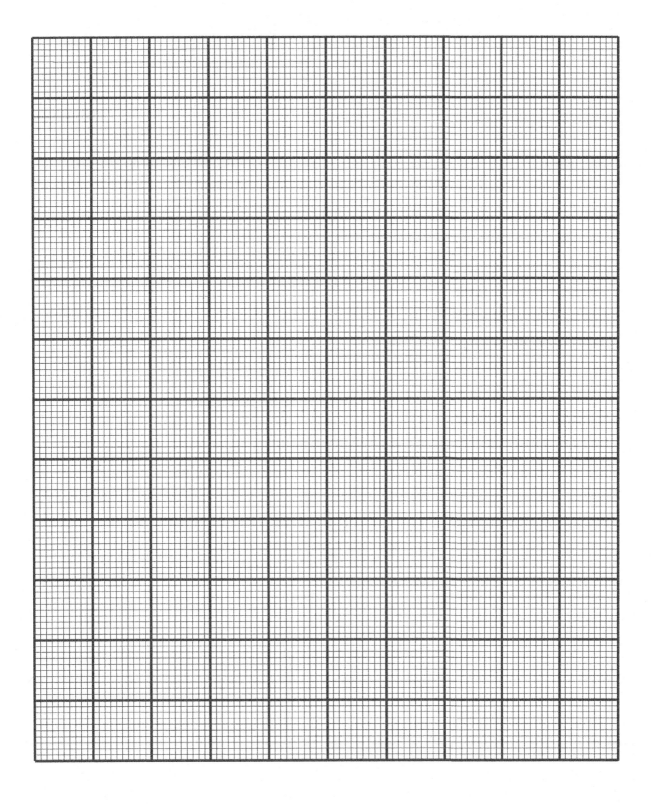

Floss Chart

STRAND	TYPE	NUMBER	COLOR	ALTERNATE

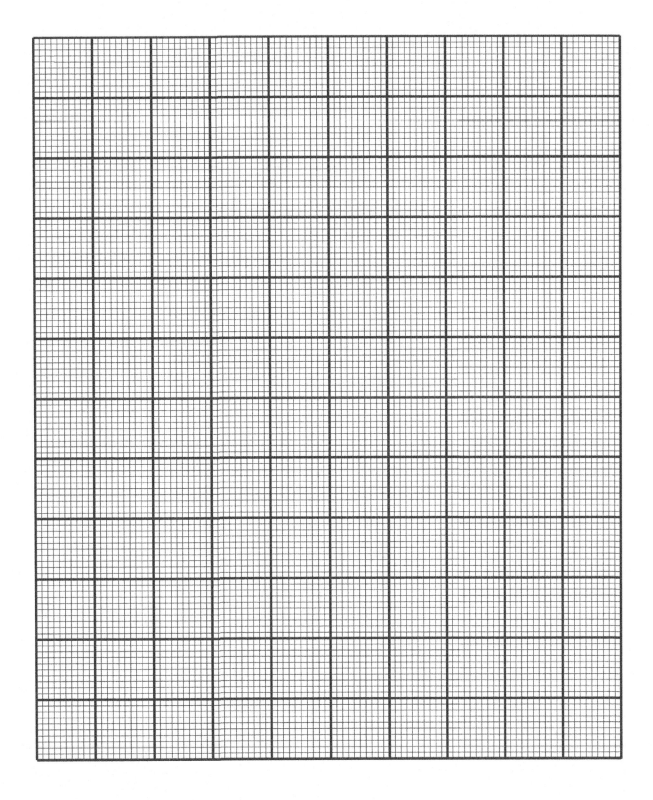

Floss Chart

STRAND	TYPE	NUMBER	COLOR	ALTERNATE

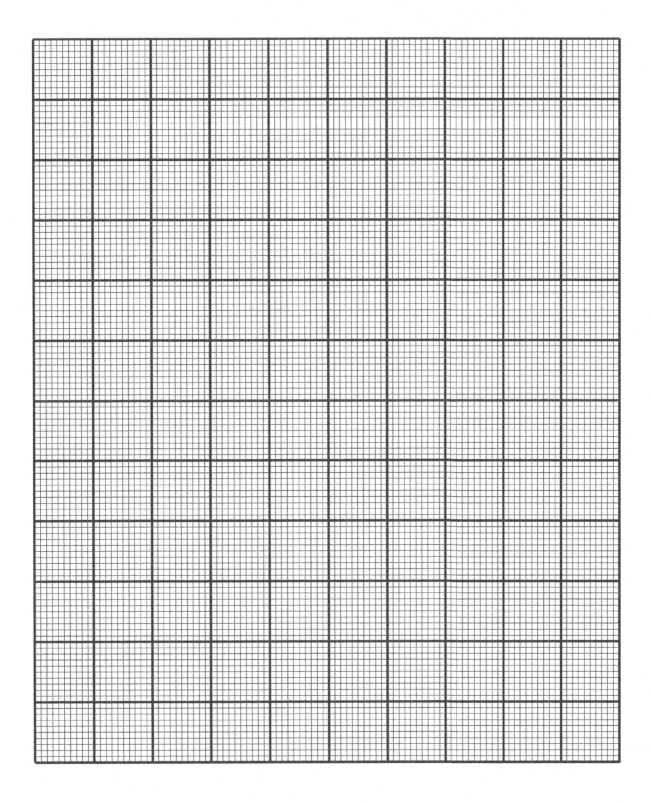

Floss Chart

STRAND	TYPE	NUMBER	COLOR	ALTERNATE

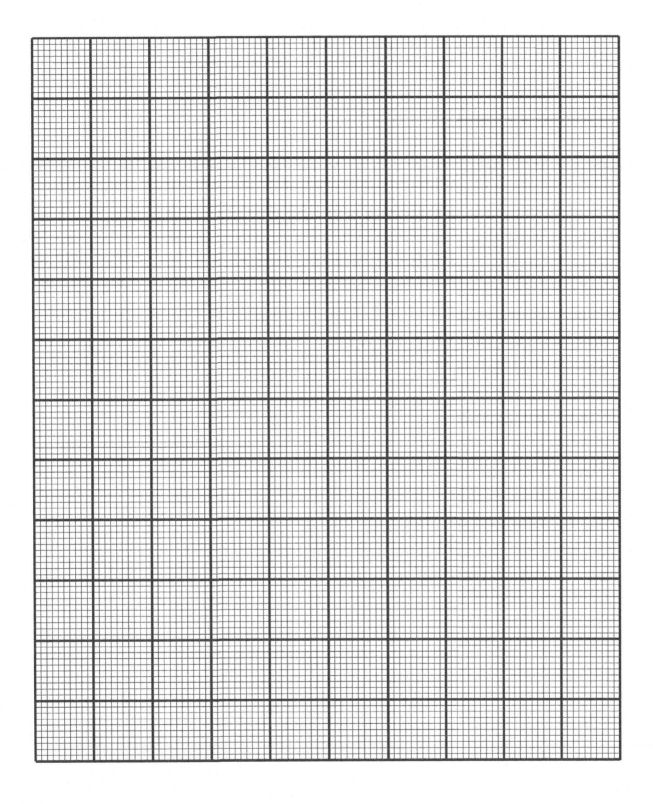

Floss Chart

STRAND	TYPE	NUMBER	COLOR	ALTERNATE

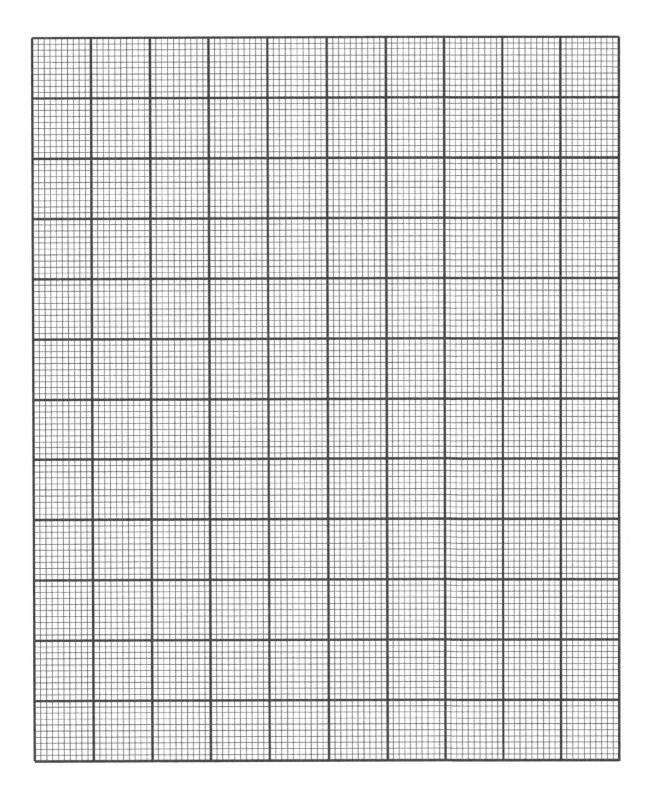

Floss Chart

STRAND	TYPE	NUMBER	COLOR	ALTERNATE

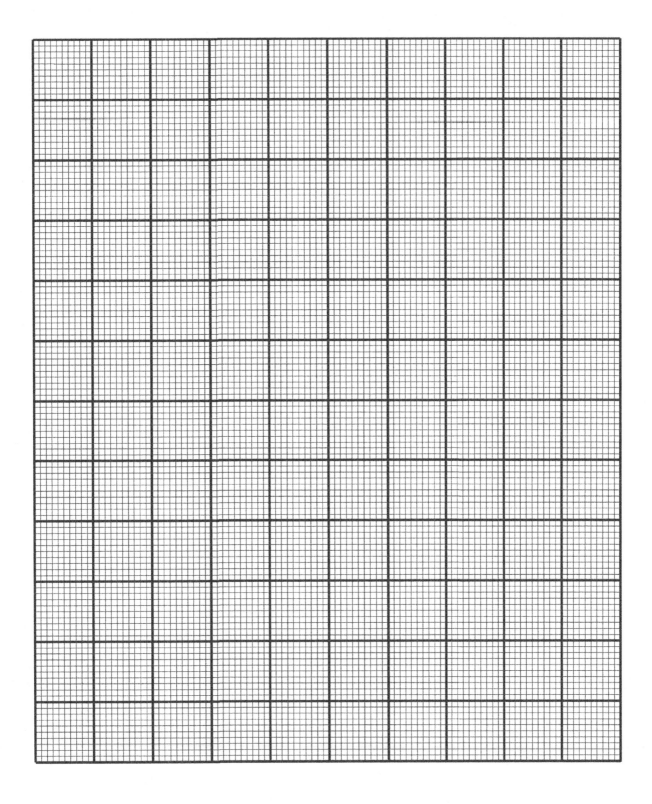

Floss Chart

STRAND	TYPE	NUMBER	COLOR	ALTERNATE

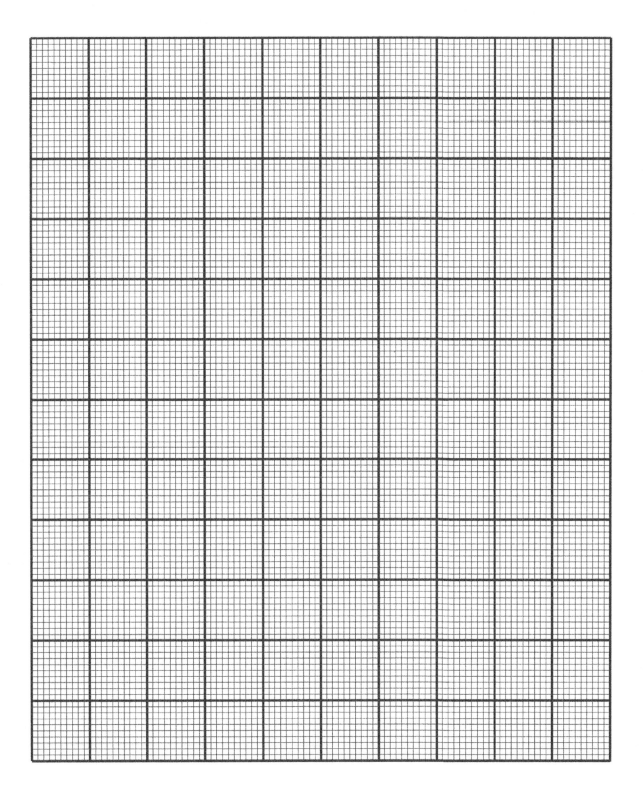

Floss Chart

STRAND	TYPE	NUMBER	COLOR	ALTERNATE

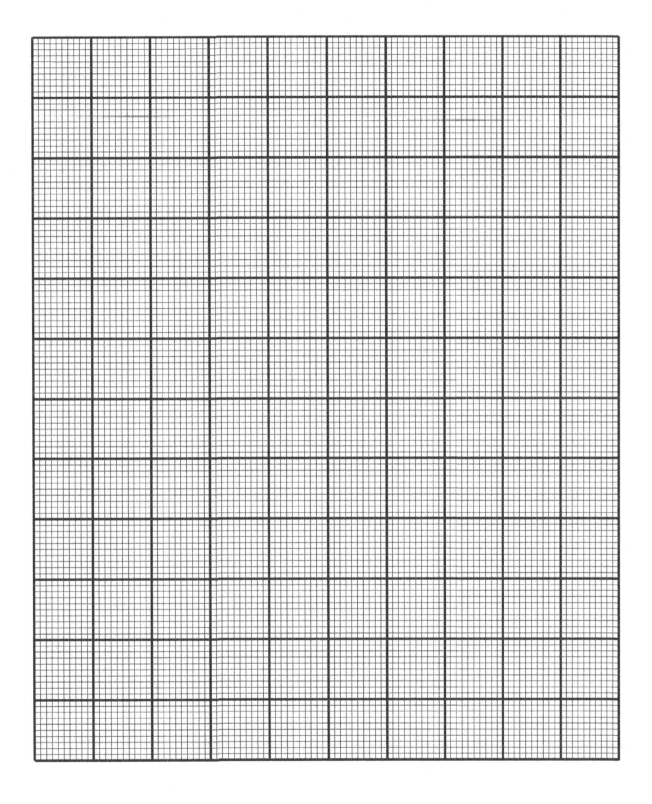

Floss Chart

STRAND	TYPE	NUMBER	COLOR	ALTERNATE

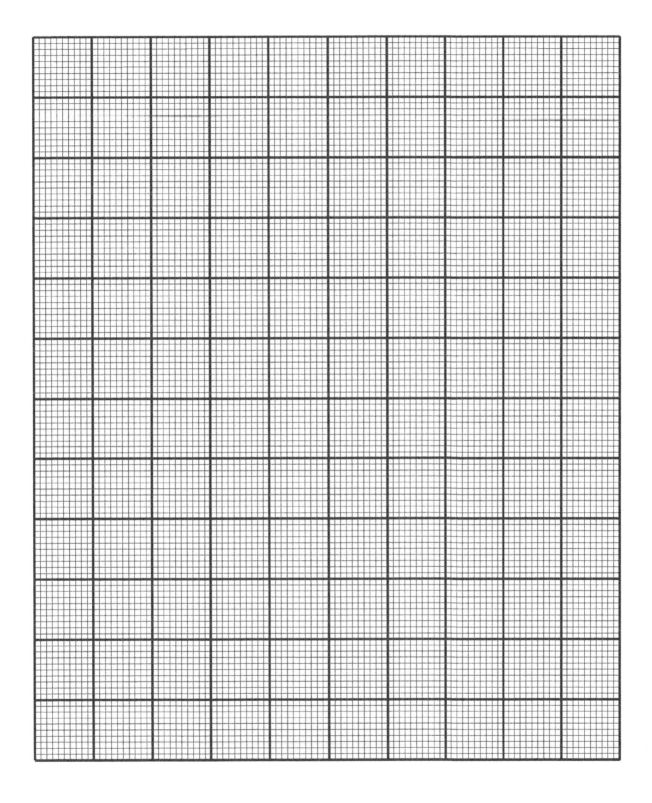

Floss Chart

STRAND	TYPE	NUMBER	COLOR	ALTERNATE

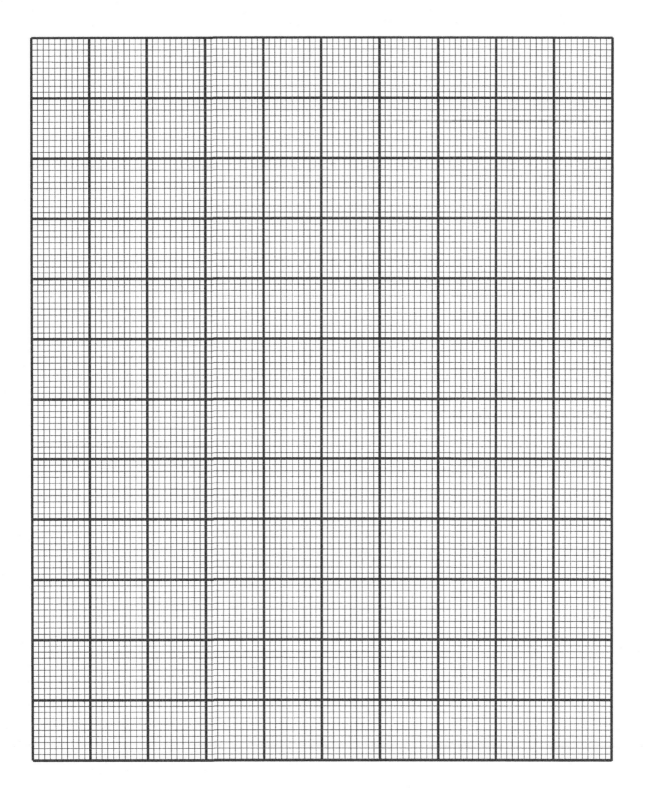

Floss Chart

STRAND	TYPE	NUMBER	COLOR	ALTERNATE

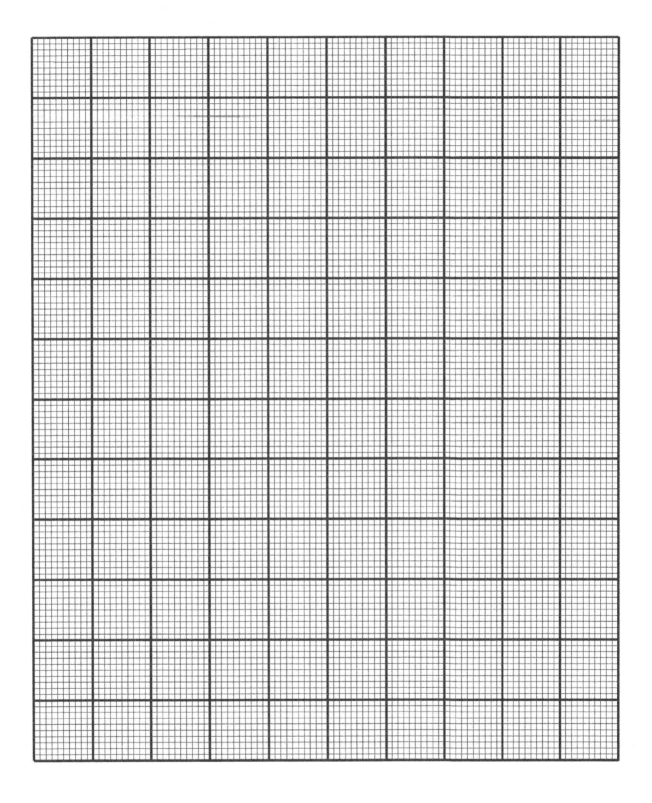

Floss Chart

STRAND	TYPE	NUMBER	COLOR	ALTERNATE

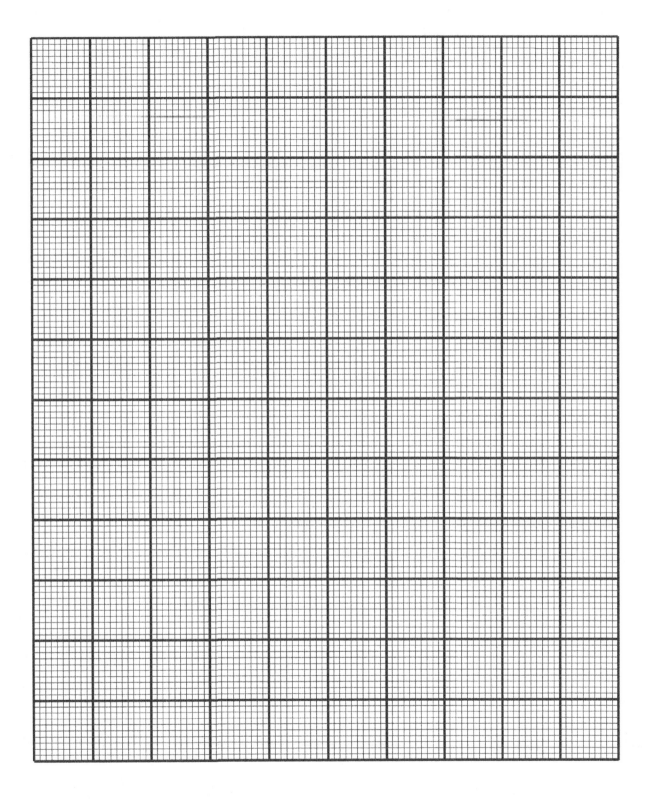

Floss Chart

STRAND	TYPE	NUMBER	COLOR	ALTERNATE

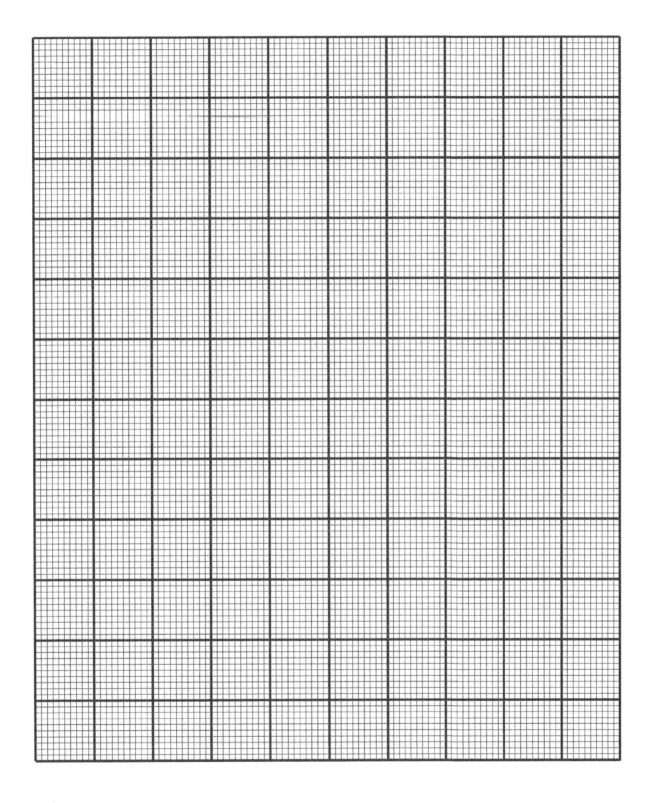

Floss Chart

STRAND	TYPE	NUMBER	COLOR	ALTERNATE

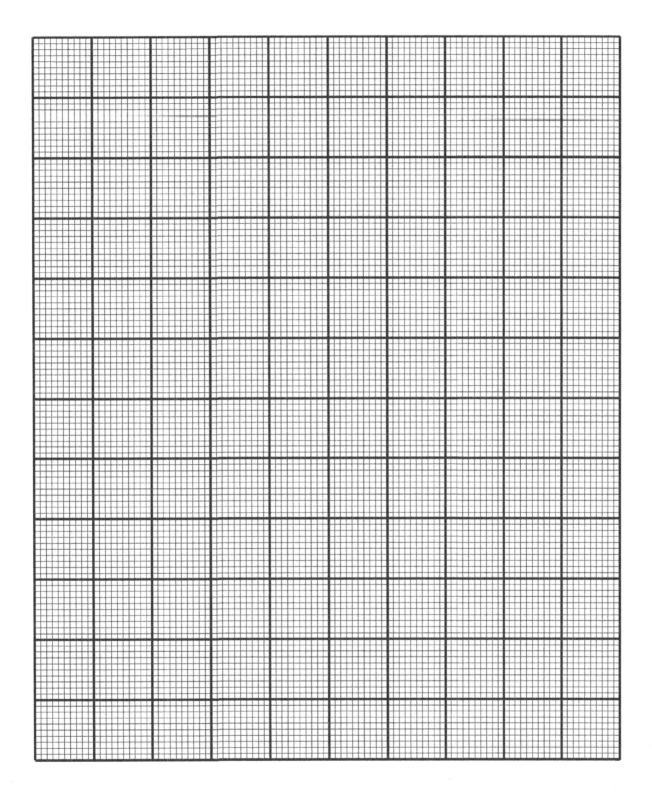

Floss Chart

STRAND	TYPE	NUMBER	COLOR	ALTERNATE

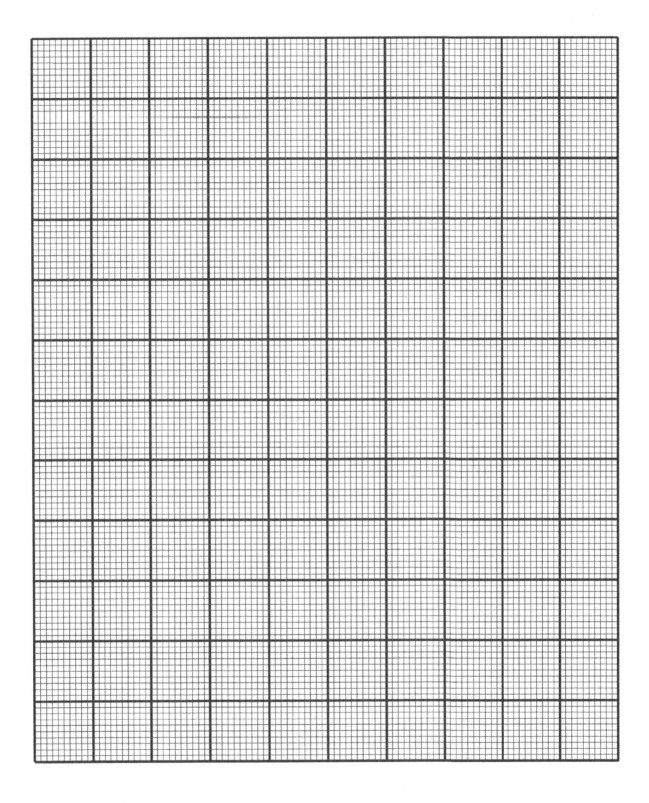

Floss Chart

STRAND	TYPE	NUMBER	COLOR	ALTERNATE

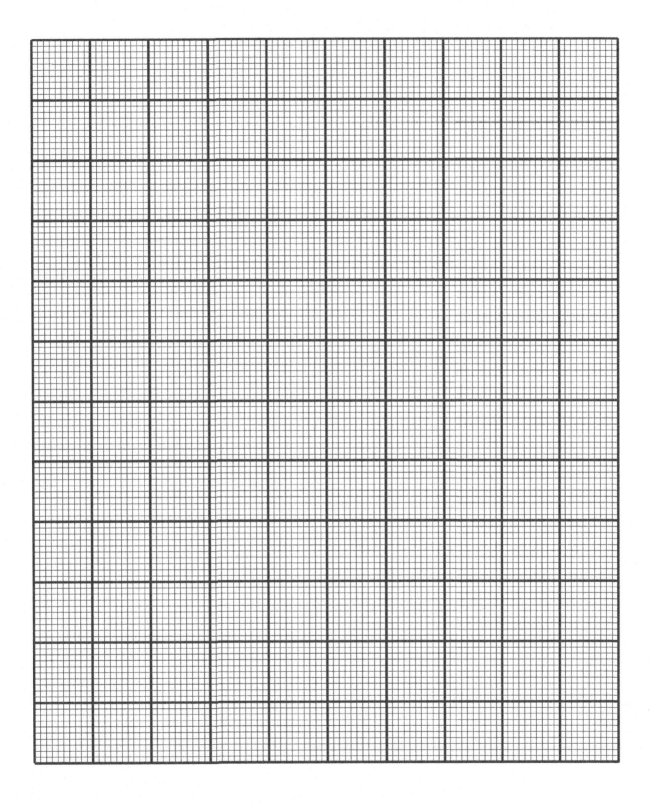

Floss Chart

STRAND	TYPE	NUMBER	COLOR	ALTERNATE

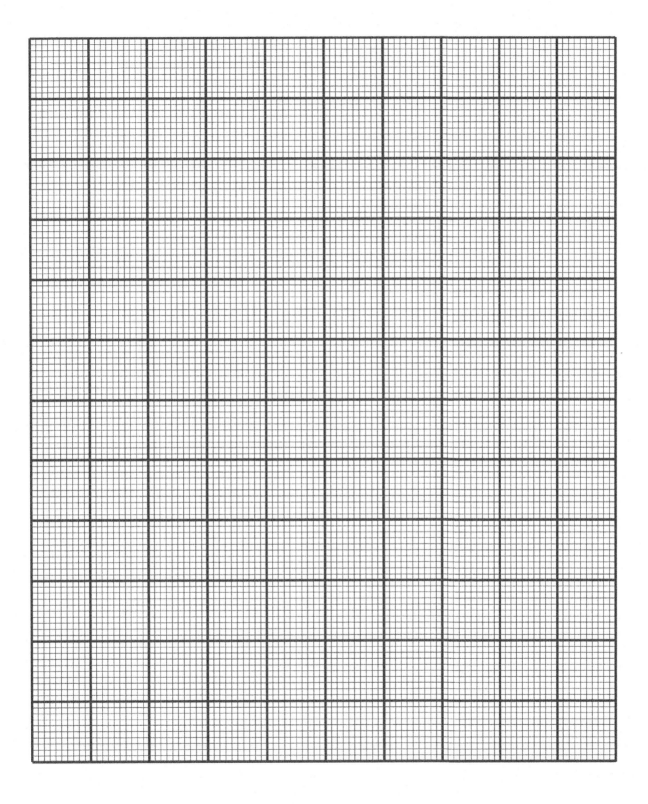

Floss Chart

STRAND	TYPE	NUMBER	COLOR	ALTERNATE

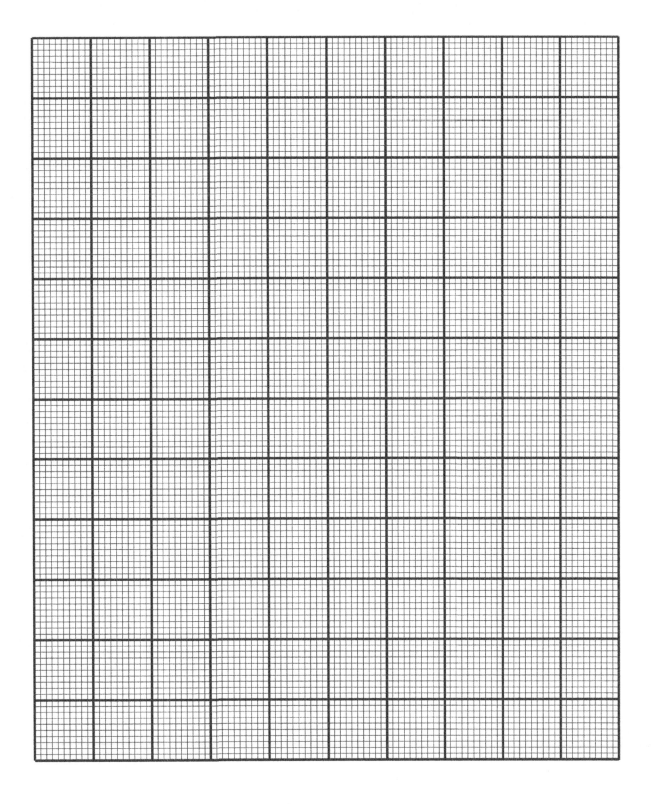

80 X 100
Stitch Count

10-Square Graph Grids

Floss Chart

STRAND	TYPE	NUMBER	COLOR	ALTERNATE

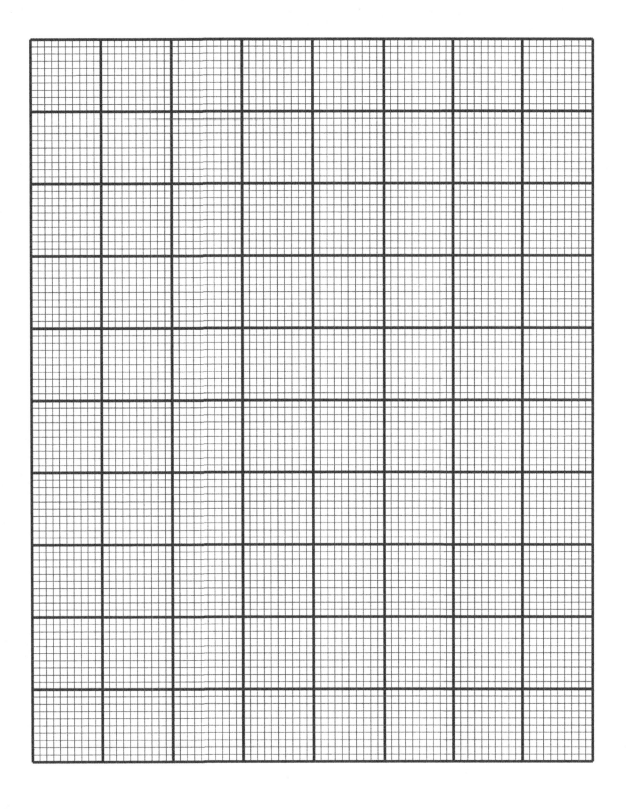

Floss Chart

STRAND	TYPE	NUMBER	COLOR	ALTERNATE

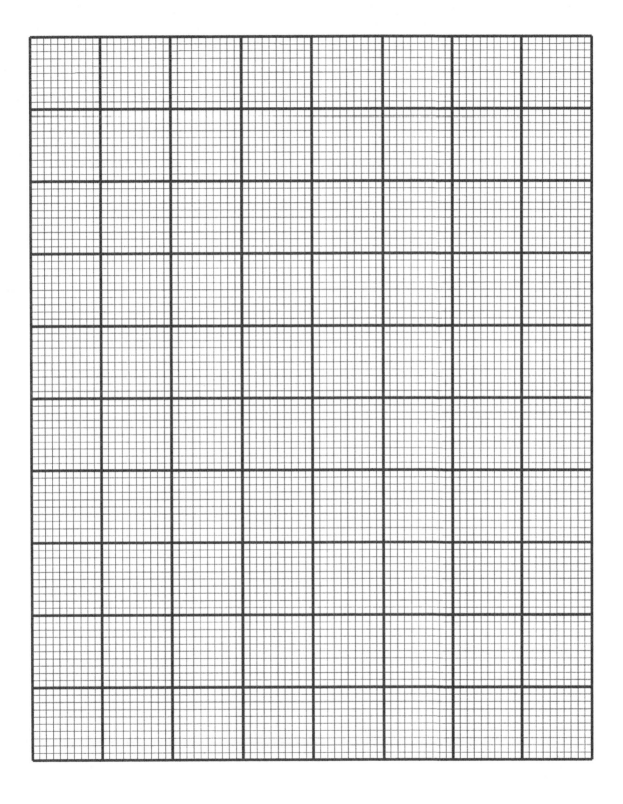

Floss Chart

STRAND	TYPE	NUMBER	COLOR	ALTERNATE

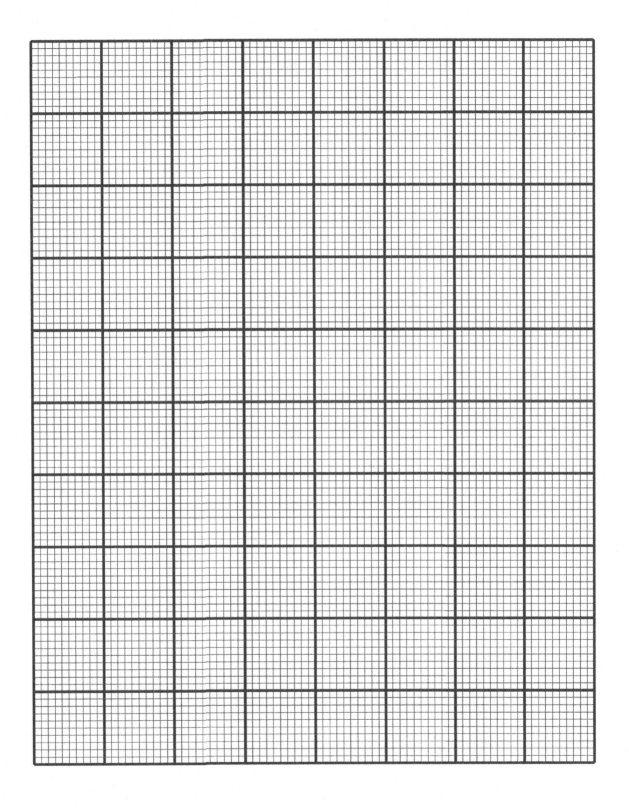

Floss Chart

STRAND	TYPE	NUMBER	COLOR	ALTERNATE

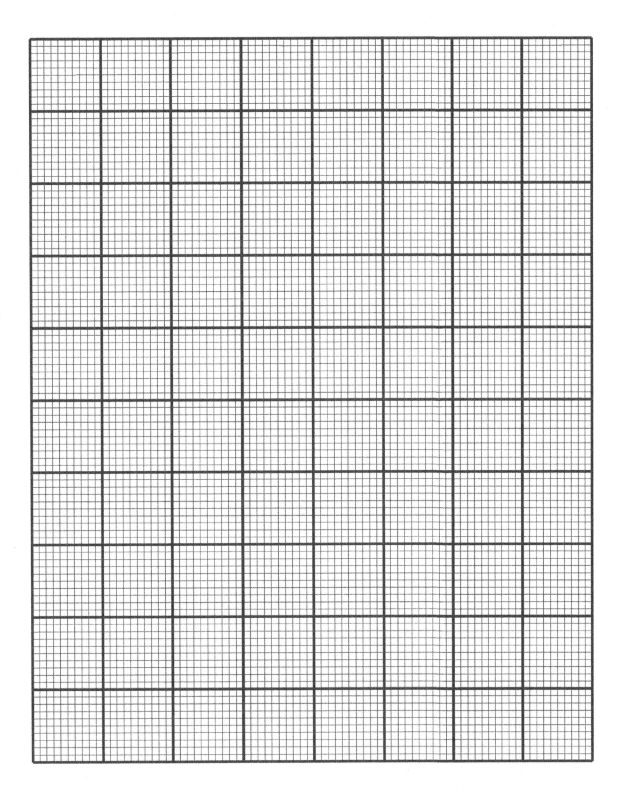

Floss Chart

STRAND	TYPE	NUMBER	COLOR	ALTERNATE

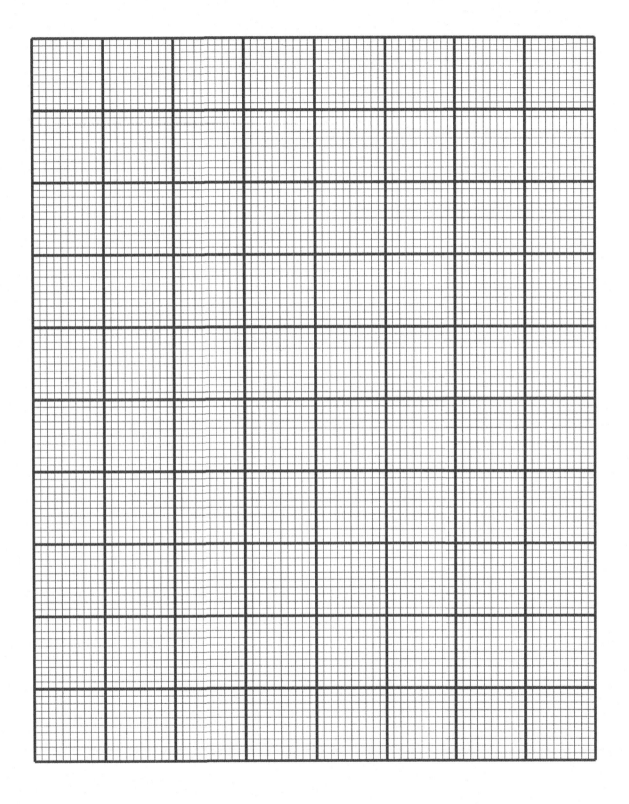

Floss Chart

STRAND	TYPE	NUMBER	COLOR	ALTERNATE

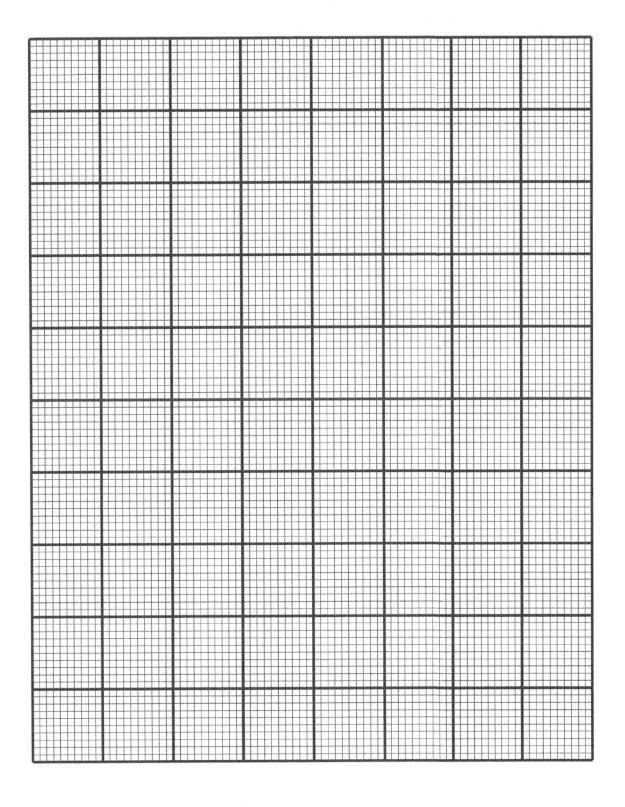

Floss Chart

STRAND	TYPE	NUMBER	COLOR	ALTERNATE

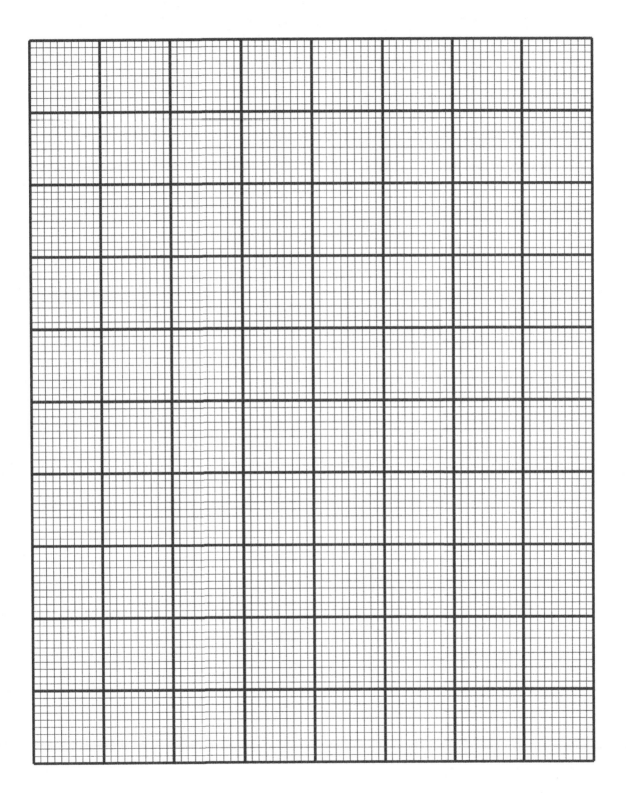

Floss Chart

STRAND	TYPE	NUMBER	COLOR	ALTERNATE

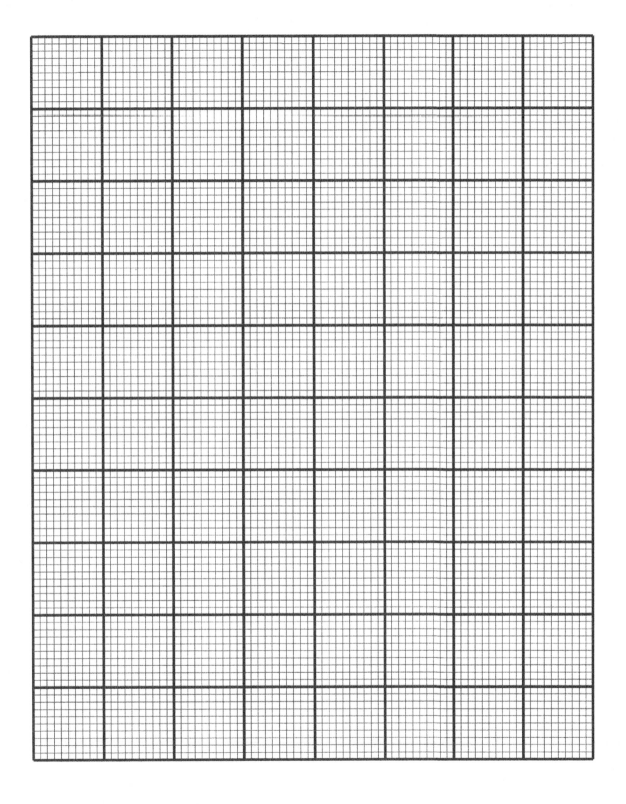

Floss Chart

STRAND	TYPE	NUMBER	COLOR	ALTERNATE

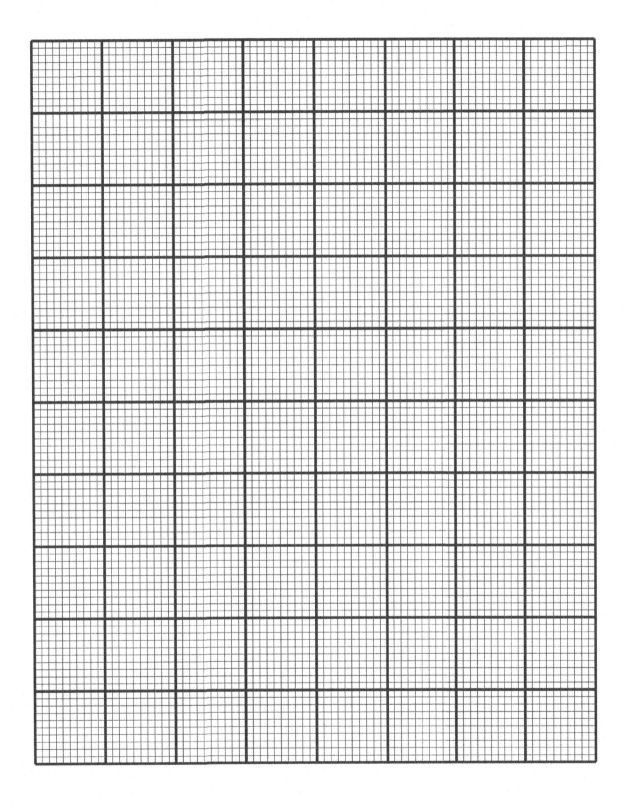

Floss Chart

STRAND	TYPE	NUMBER	COLOR	ALTERNATE

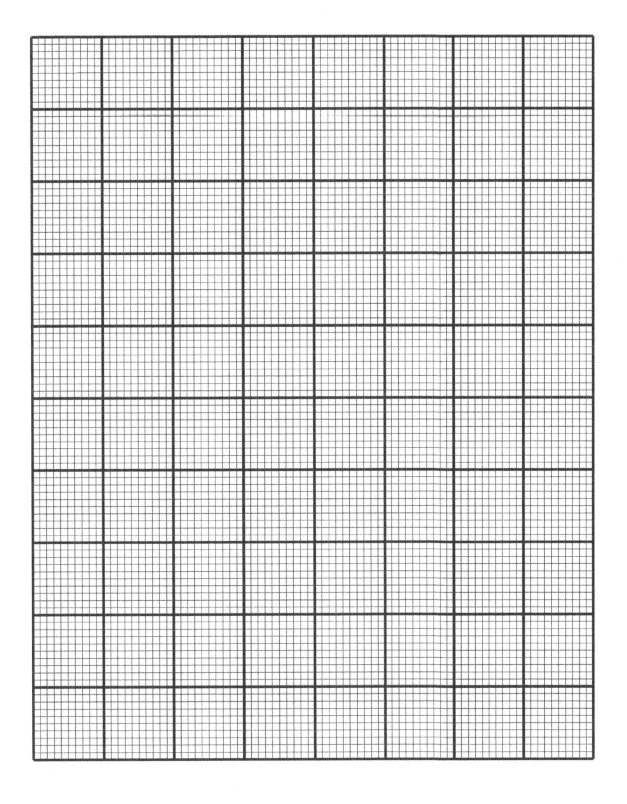

Floss Chart

STRAND	TYPE	NUMBER	COLOR	ALTERNATE

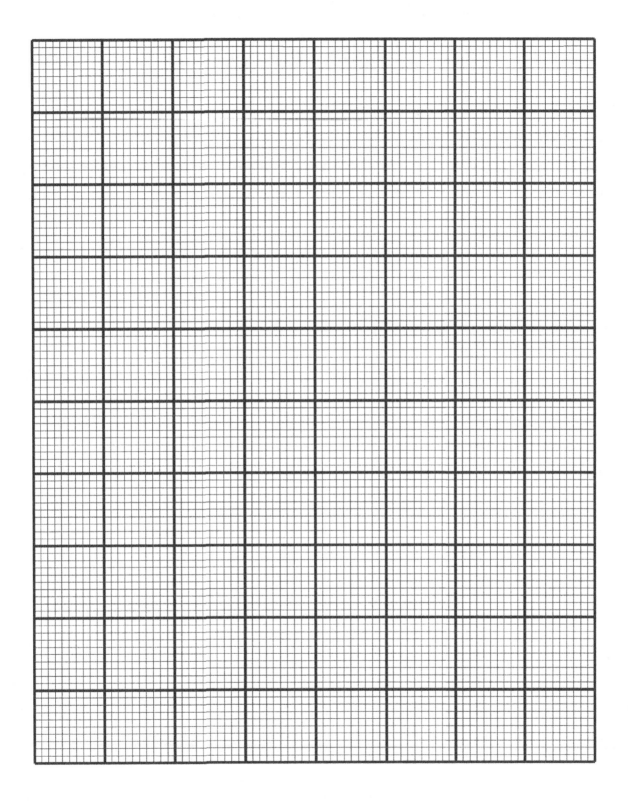

Floss Chart

STRAND	TYPE	NUMBER	COLOR	ALTERNATE

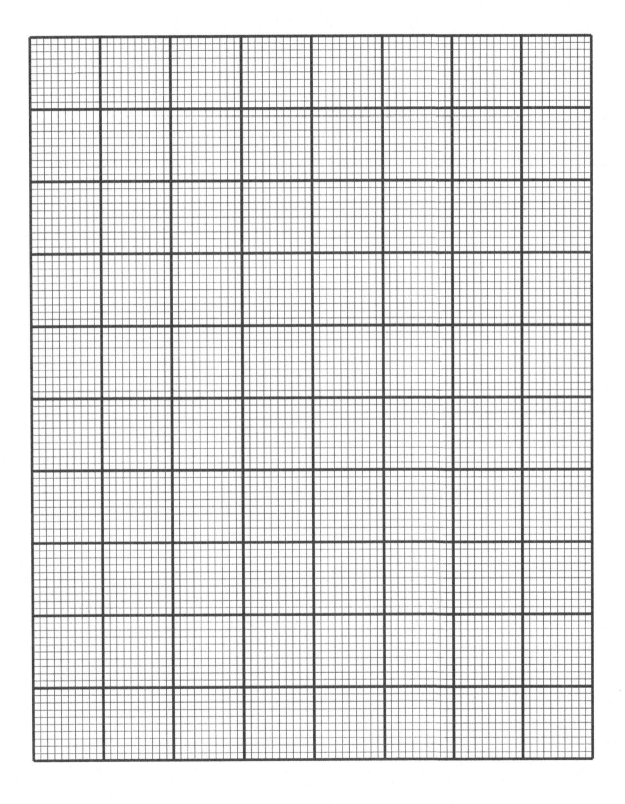

Floss Chart

STRAND	TYPE	NUMBER	COLOR	ALTERNATE

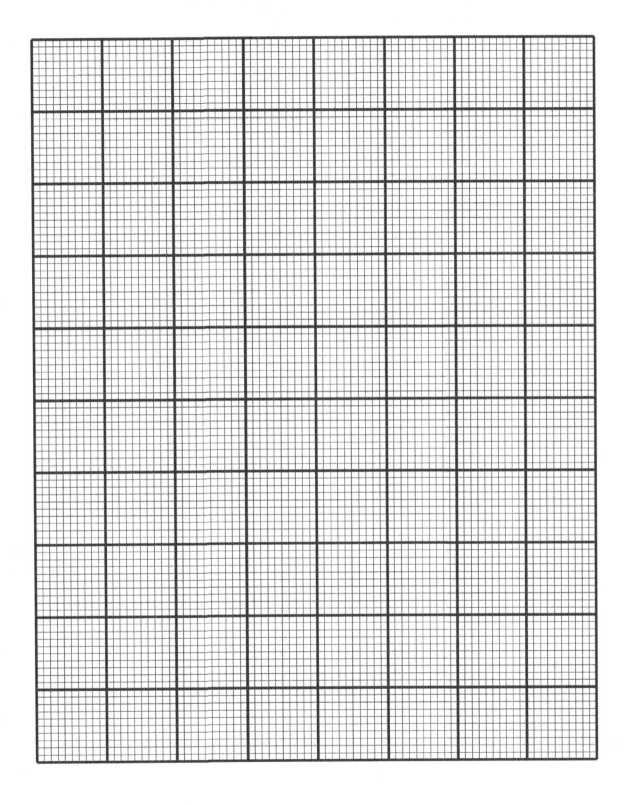

Floss Chart

STRAND	TYPE	NUMBER	COLOR	ALTERNATE

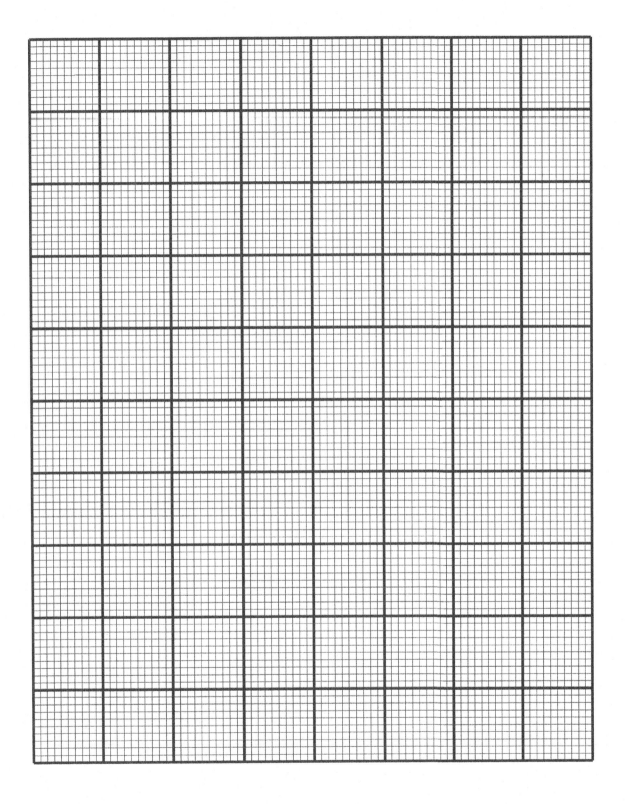

Floss Chart

STRAND	TYPE	NUMBER	COLOR	ALTERNATE

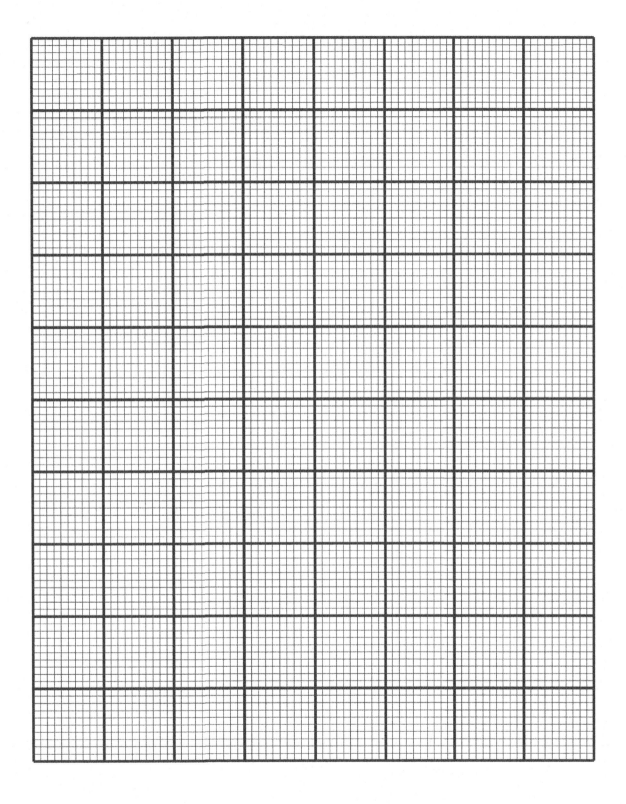

Floss Chart

STRAND	TYPE	NUMBER	COLOR	ALTERNATE

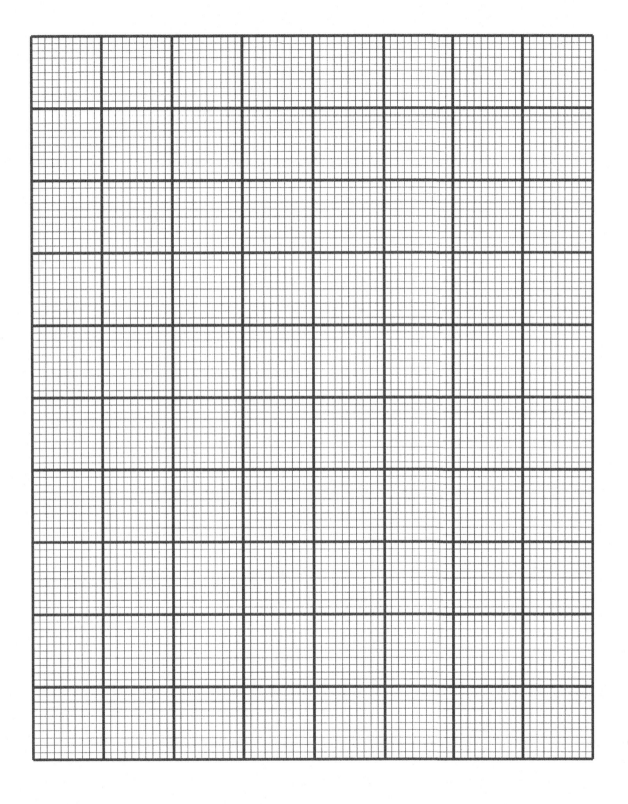

Floss Chart

STRAND	TYPE	NUMBER	COLOR	ALTERNATE

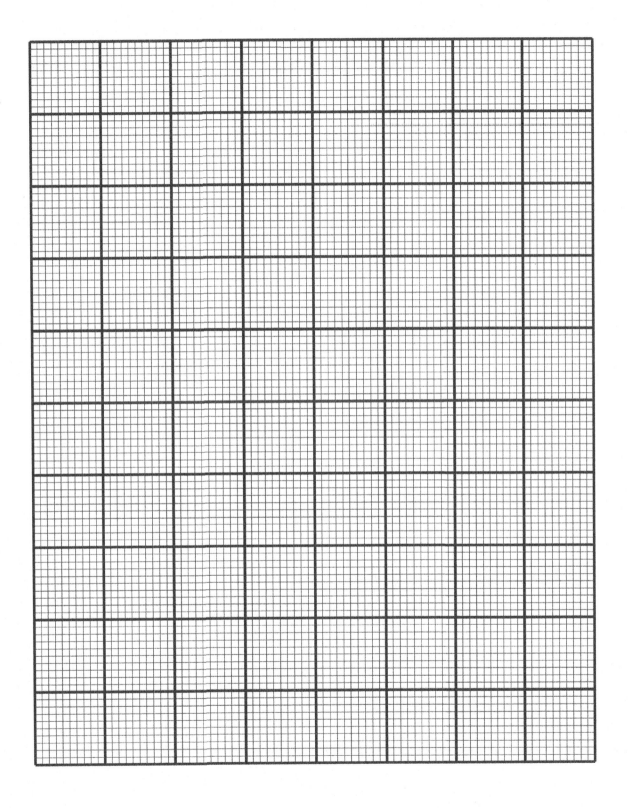

Floss Chart

STRAND	TYPE	NUMBER	COLOR	ALTERNATE

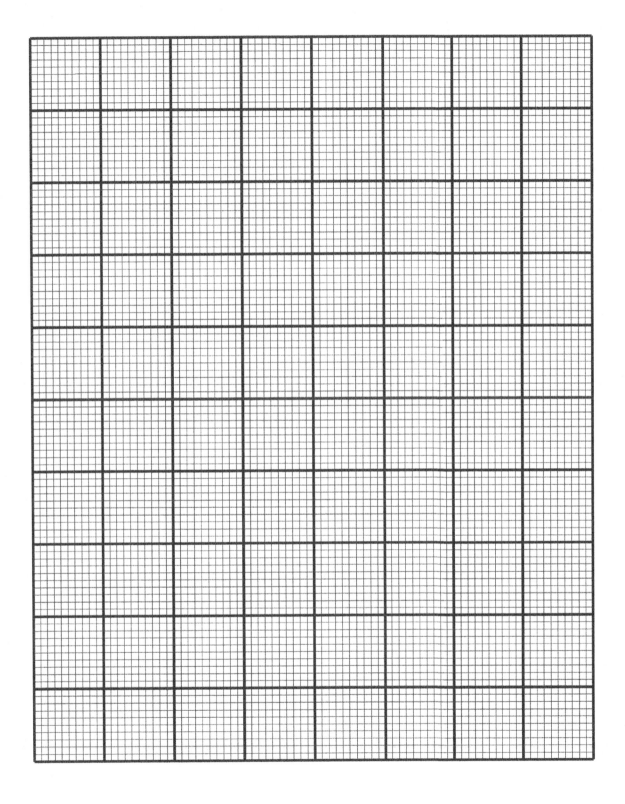

Floss Chart

STRAND	TYPE	NUMBER	COLOR	ALTERNATE

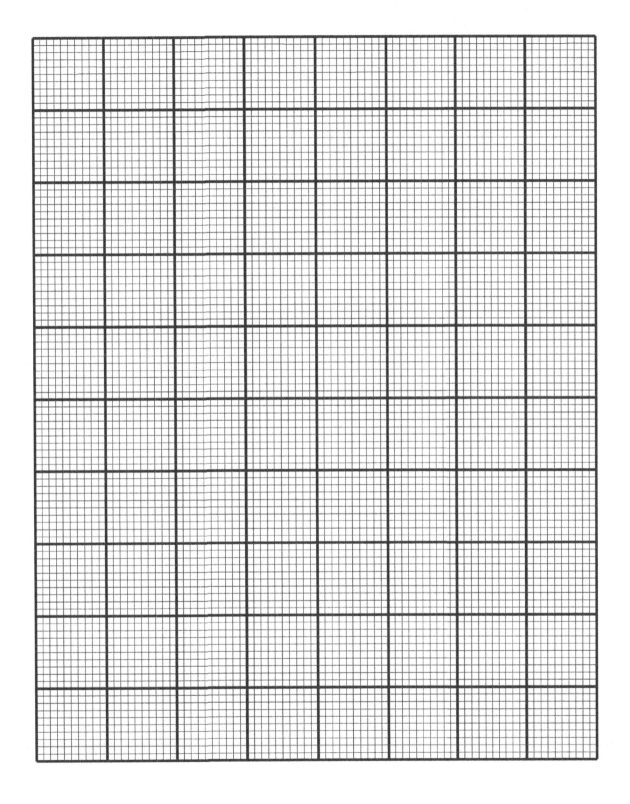

Floss Chart

STRAND	TYPE	NUMBER	COLOR	ALTERNATE

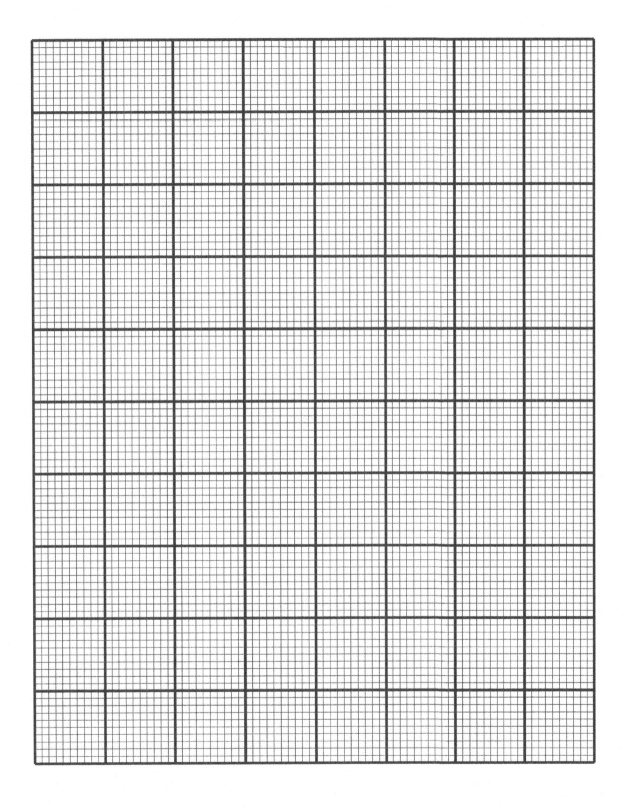

60 X 80
Stitch Count

10-Square Graph Grids

Floss Chart

STRAND	TYPE	NUMBER	COLOR	ALTERNATE

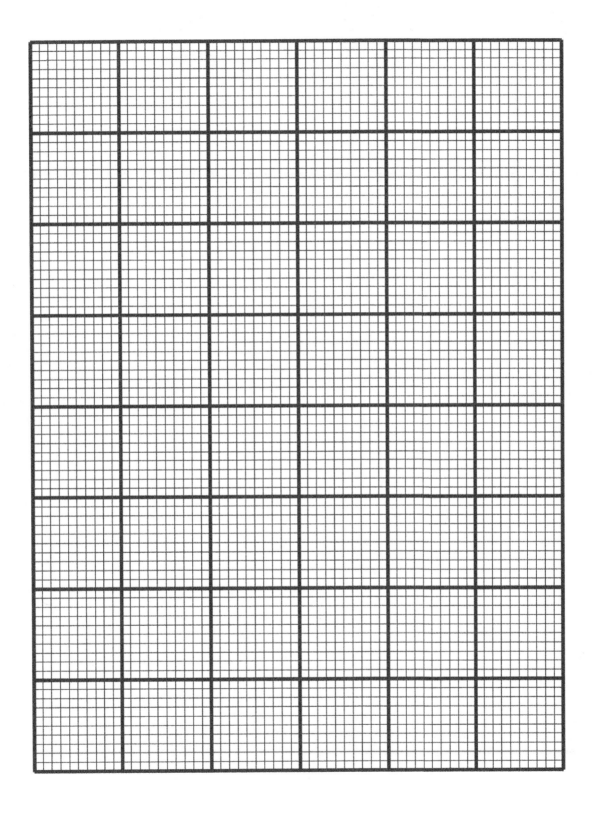

Floss Chart

STRAND	TYPE	NUMBER	COLOR	ALTERNATE

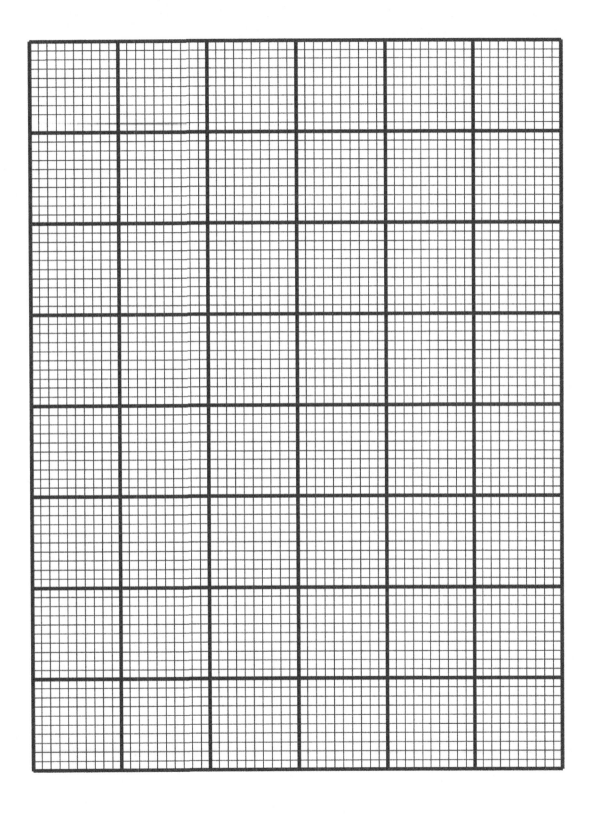

Floss Chart

STRAND	TYPE	NUMBER	COLOR	ALTERNATE

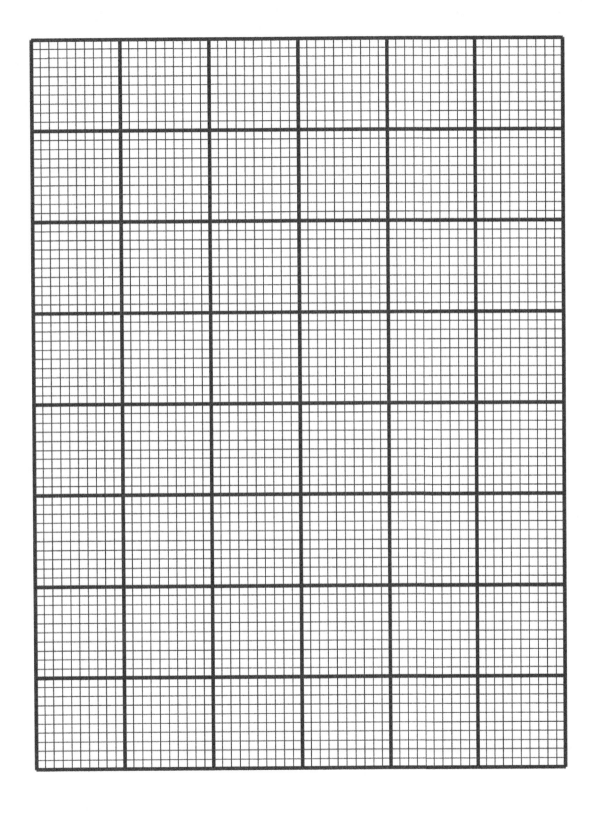

Floss Chart

STRAND	TYPE	NUMBER	COLOR	ALTERNATE

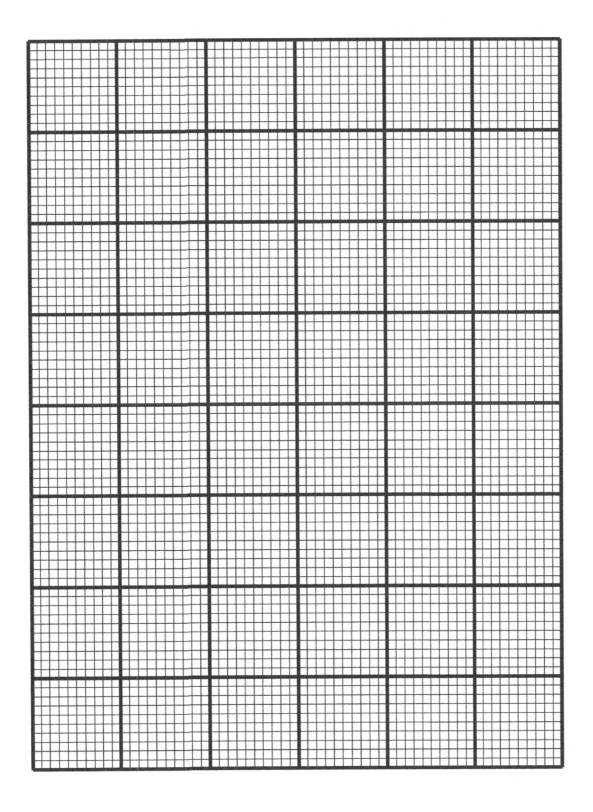

Floss Chart

STRAND	TYPE	NUMBER	COLOR	ALTERNATE

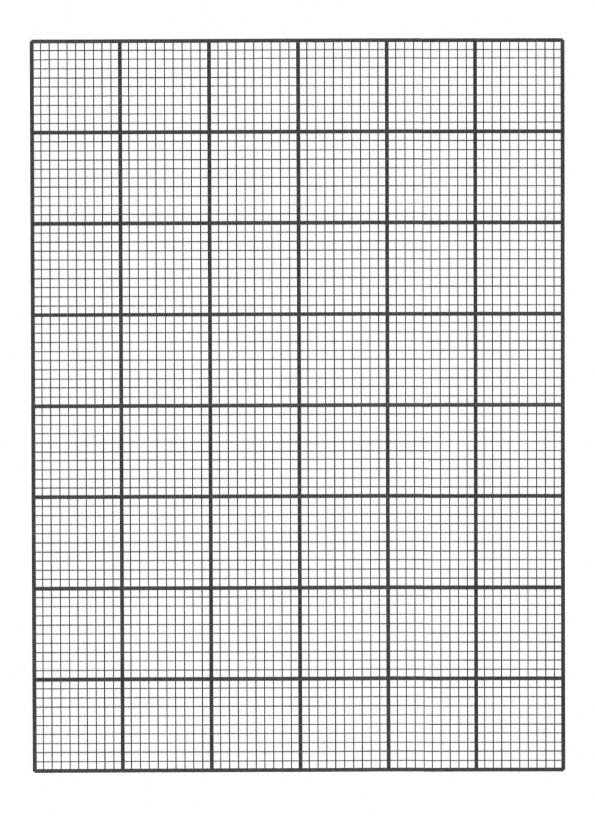

Floss Chart

STRAND	TYPE	NUMBER	COLOR	ALTERNATE

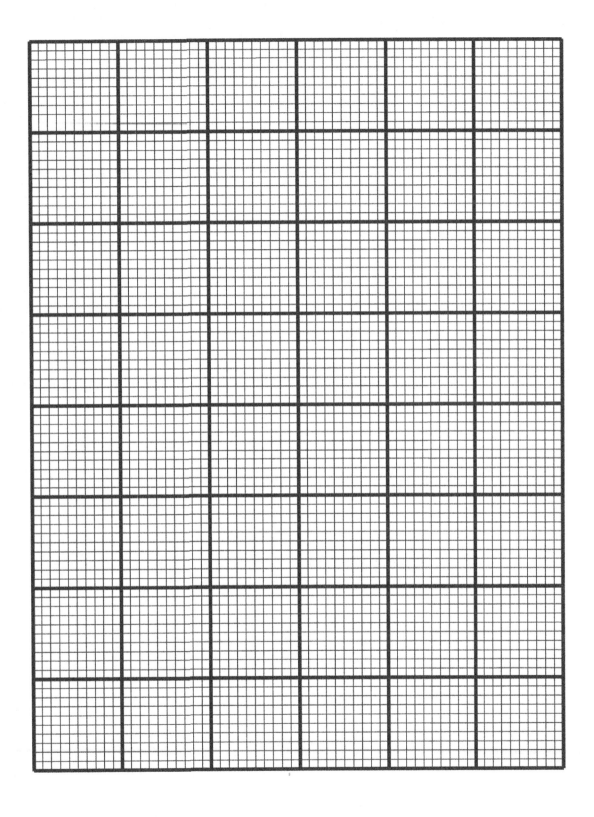

Floss Chart

STRAND	TYPE	NUMBER	COLOR	ALTERNATE

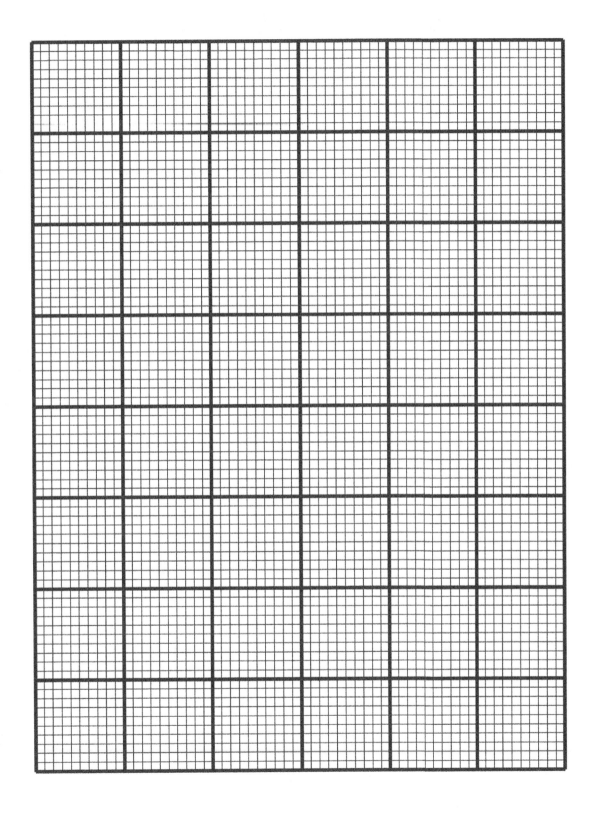

Floss Chart

STRAND	TYPE	NUMBER	COLOR	ALTERNATE

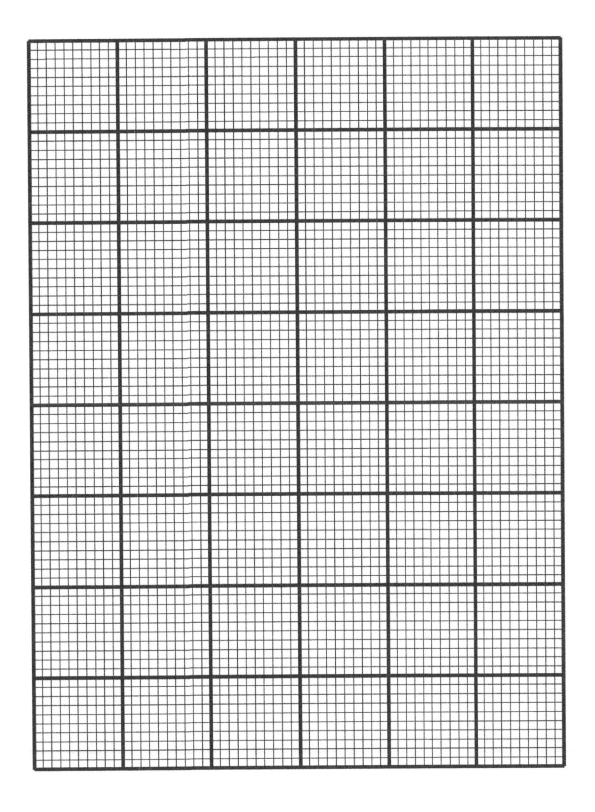

Floss Chart

STRAND	TYPE	NUMBER	COLOR	ALTERNATE

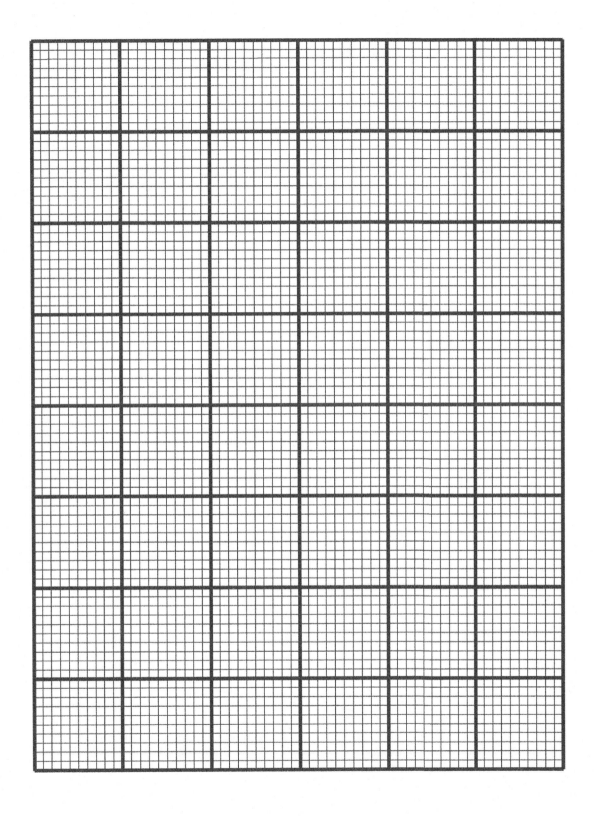

Floss Chart

STRAND	TYPE	NUMBER	COLOR	ALTERNATE

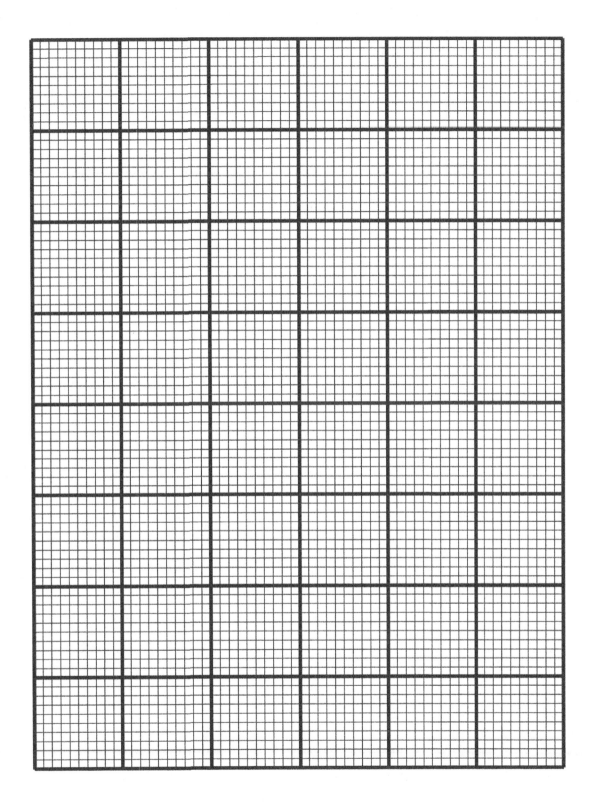

Floss Chart

STRAND	TYPE	NUMBER	COLOR	ALTERNATE

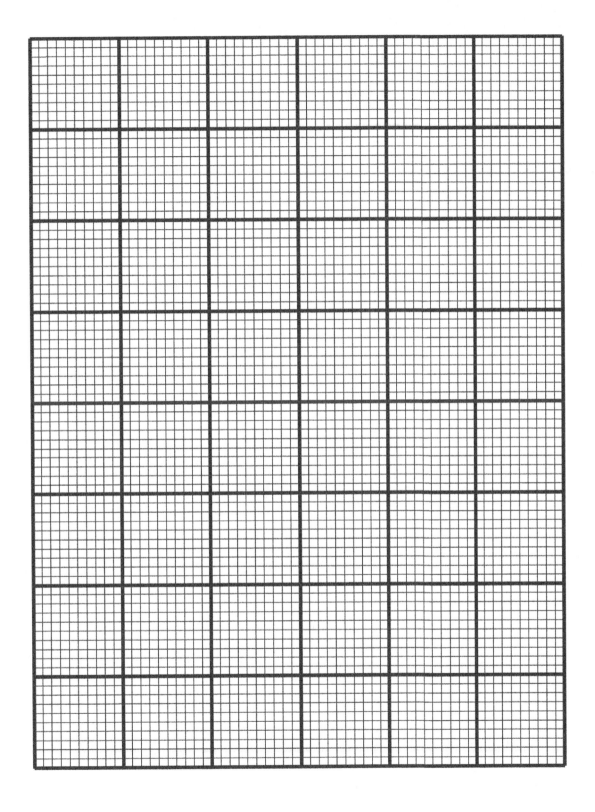

Floss Chart

STRAND	TYPE	NUMBER	COLOR	ALTERNATE

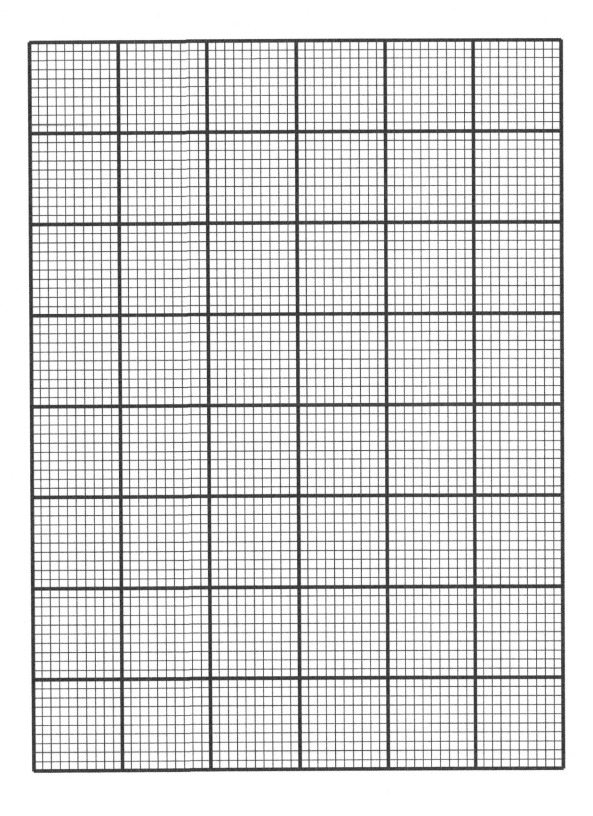

Floss Chart

STRAND	TYPE	NUMBER	COLOR	ALTERNATE

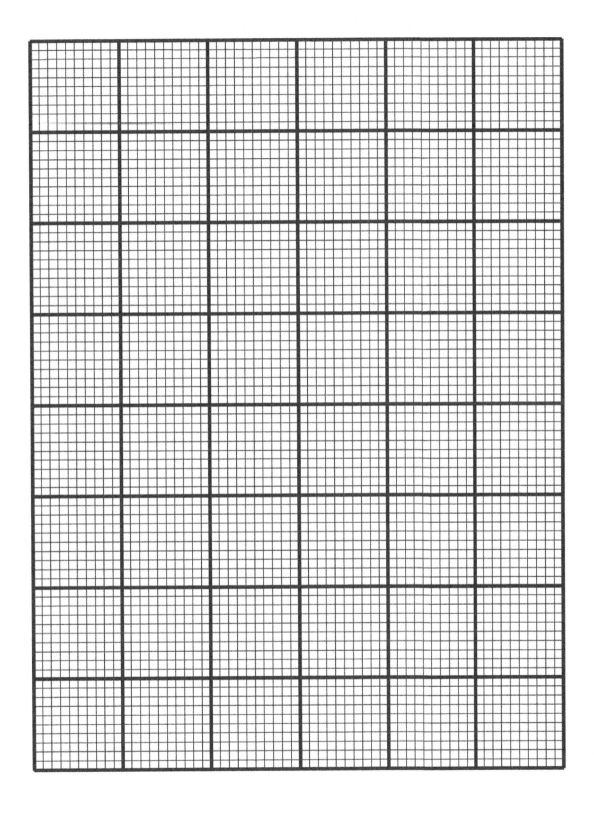

Floss Chart

STRAND	TYPE	NUMBER	COLOR	ALTERNATE

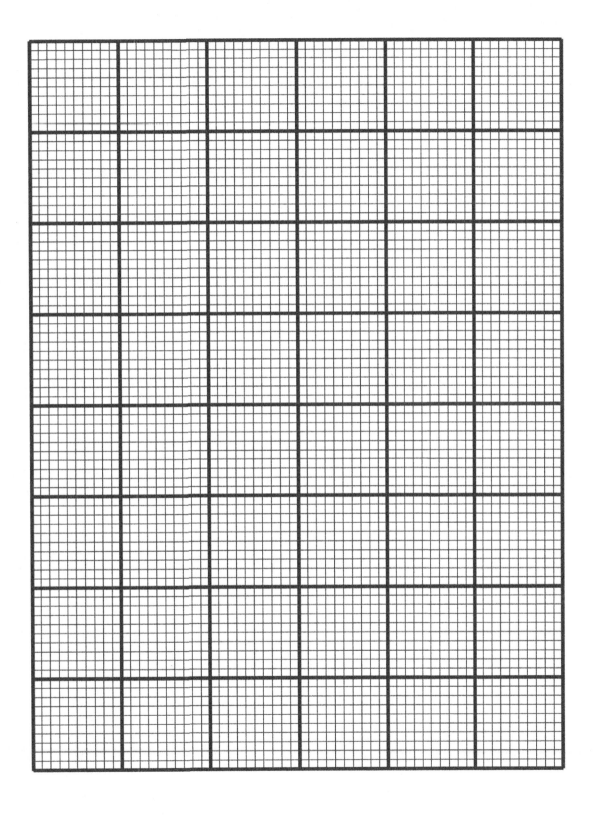

Floss Chart

STRAND	TYPE	NUMBER	COLOR	ALTERNATE

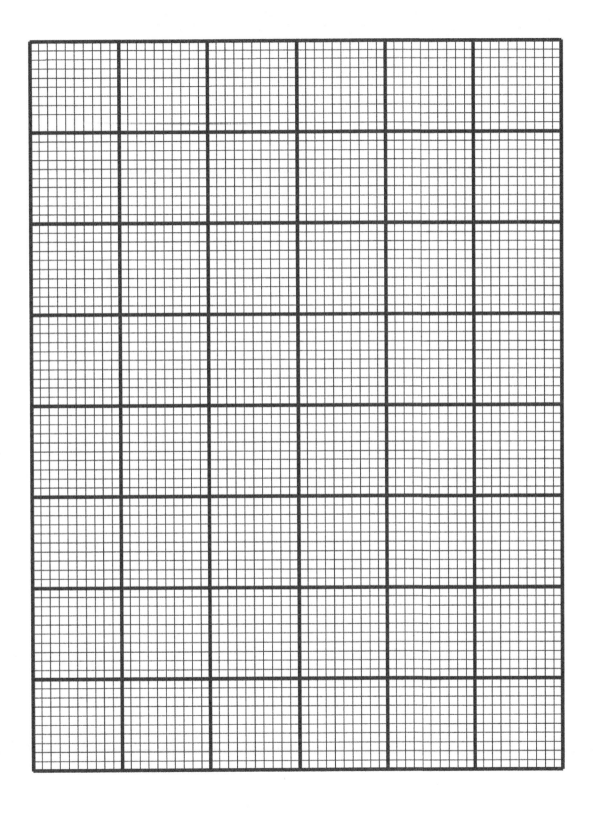

Floss Chart

	STRAND	TYPE	NUMBER	COLOR	ALTERNATE

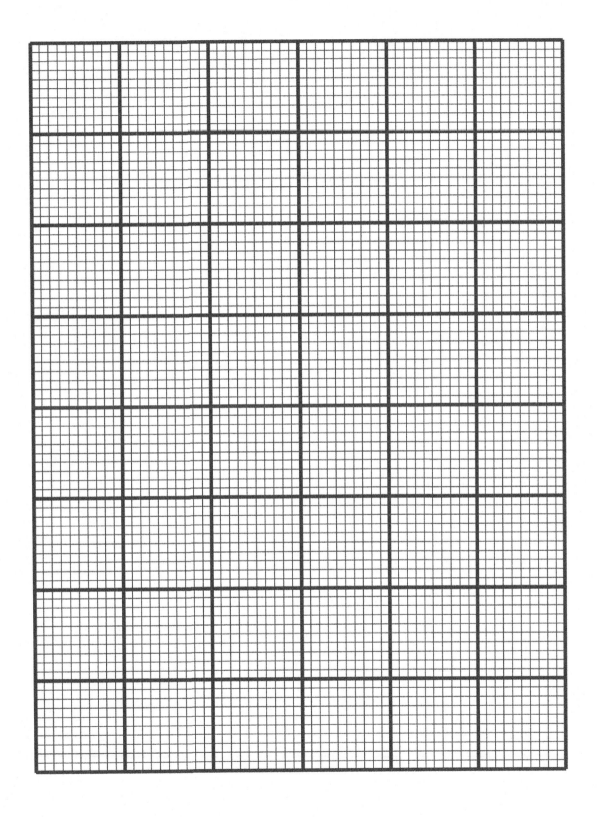

Floss Chart

STRAND	TYPE	NUMBER	COLOR	ALTERNATE

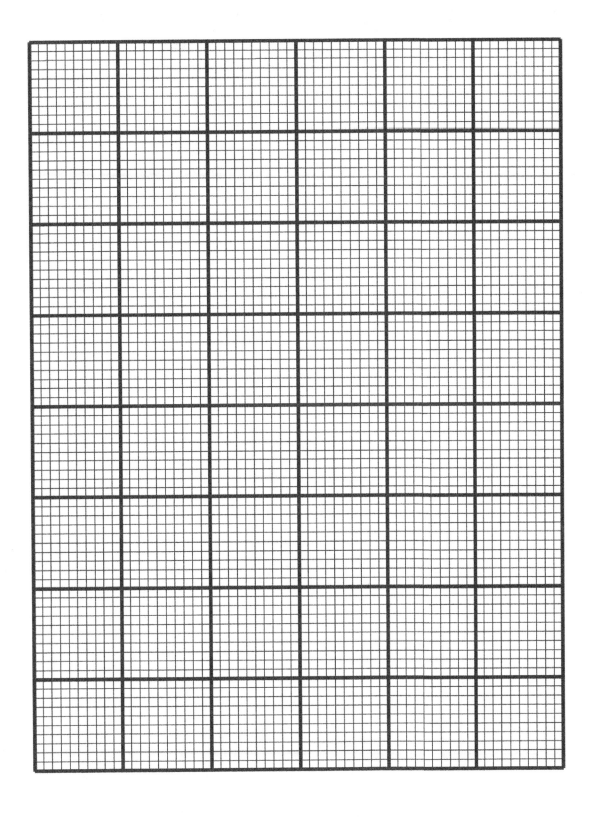

Floss Chart

STRAND	TYPE	NUMBER	COLOR	ALTERNATE

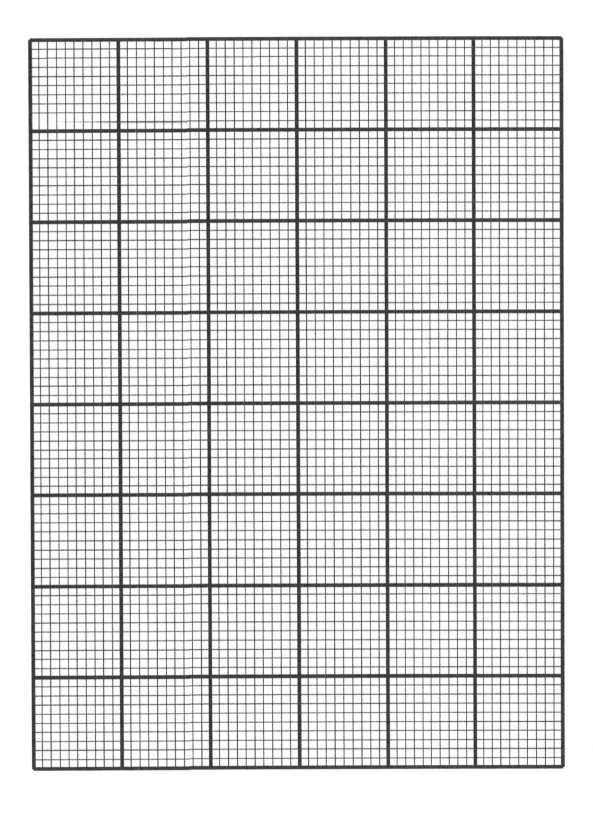

Floss Chart

STRAND	TYPE	NUMBER	COLOR	ALTERNATE

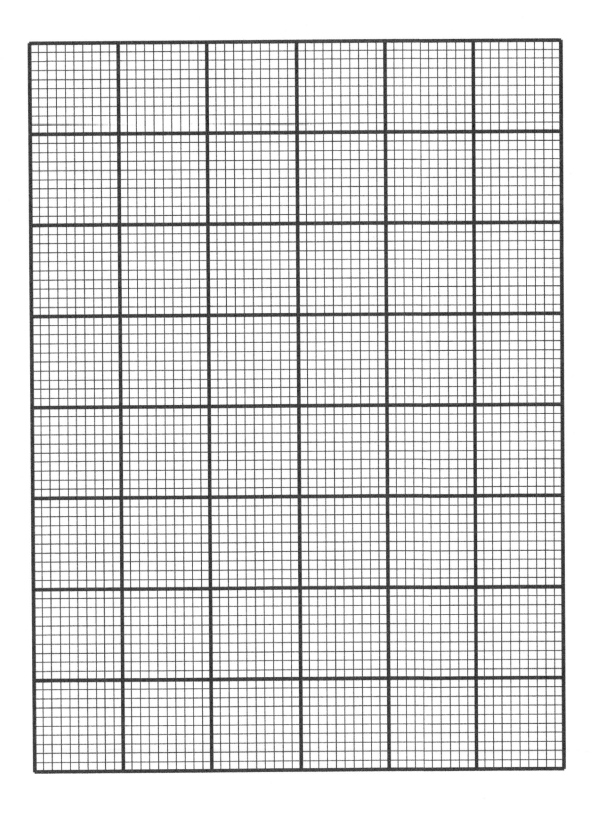

Floss Chart

STRAND	TYPE	NUMBER	COLOR	ALTERNATE

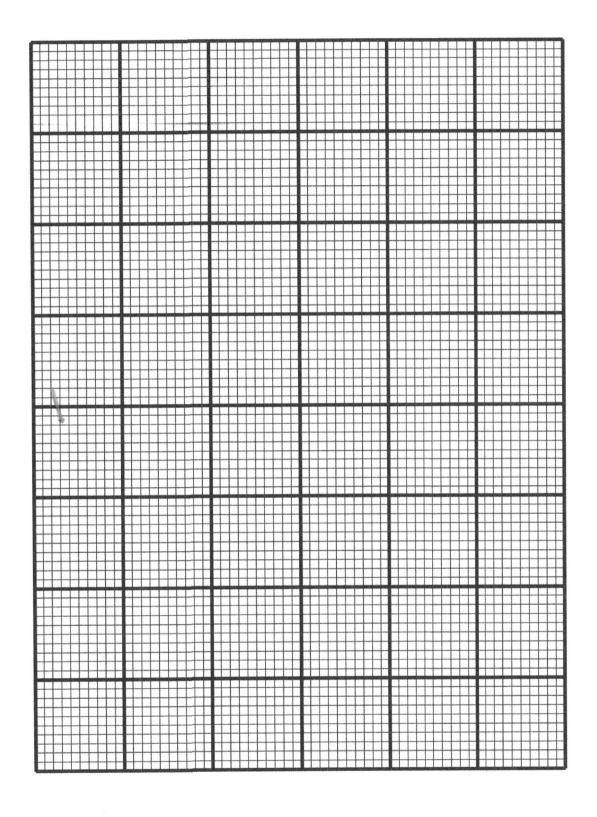

40 X 60
Stitch Count

10-Square Graph Grids

Floss Chart

STRAND	TYPE	NUMBER	COLOR	ALTERNATE

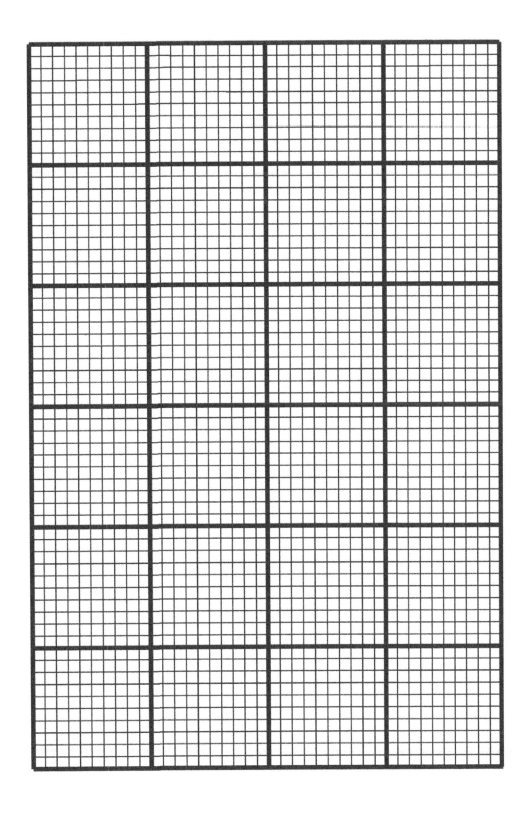

Floss Chart

STRAND	TYPE	NUMBER	COLOR	ALTERNATE

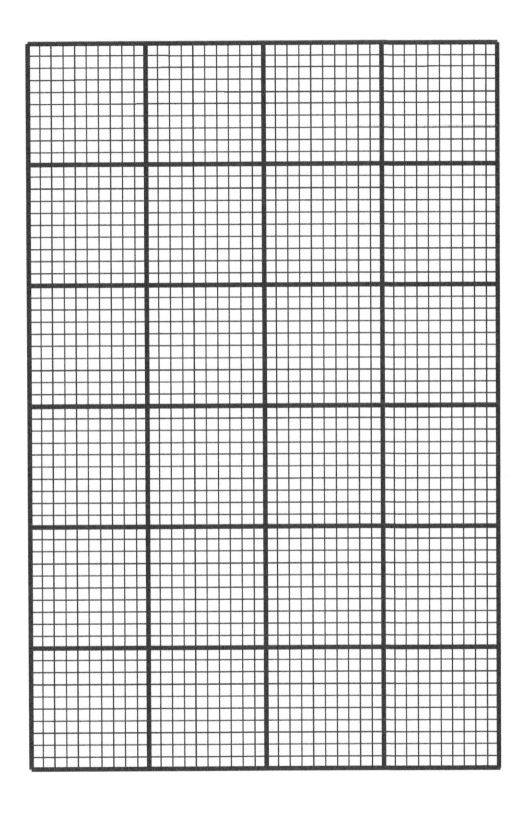

Floss Chart

STRAND	TYPE	NUMBER	COLOR	ALTERNATE

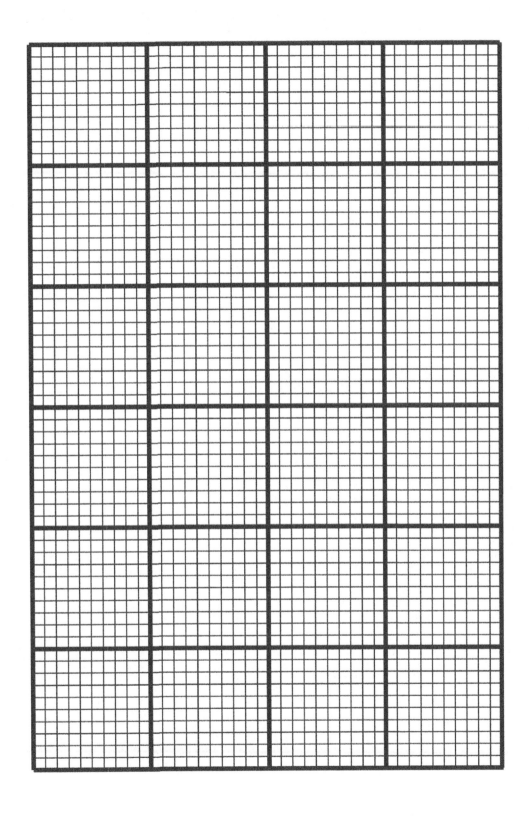

Floss Chart

STRAND	TYPE	NUMBER	COLOR	ALTERNATE

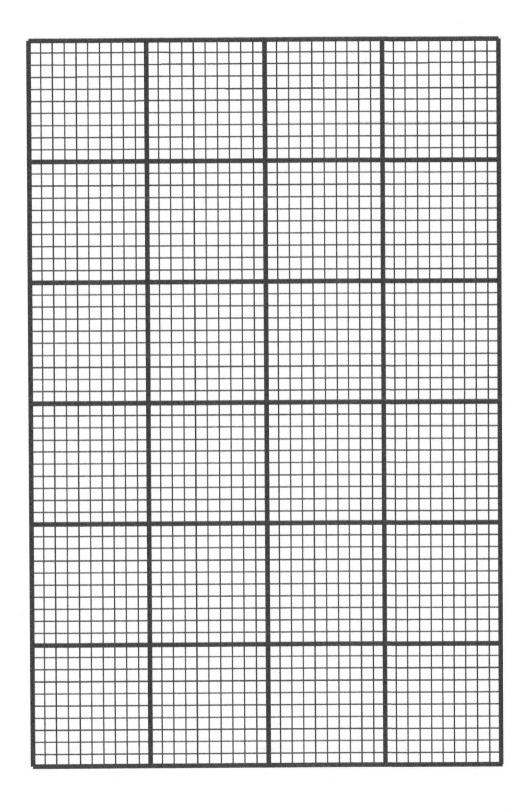

Floss Chart

STRAND	TYPE	NUMBER	COLOR	ALTERNATE

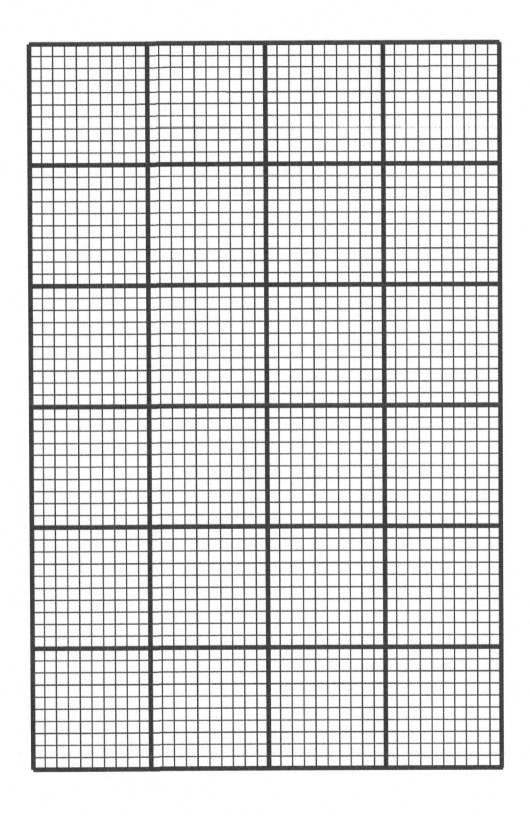

Floss Chart

STRAND	TYPE	NUMBER	COLOR	ALTERNATE

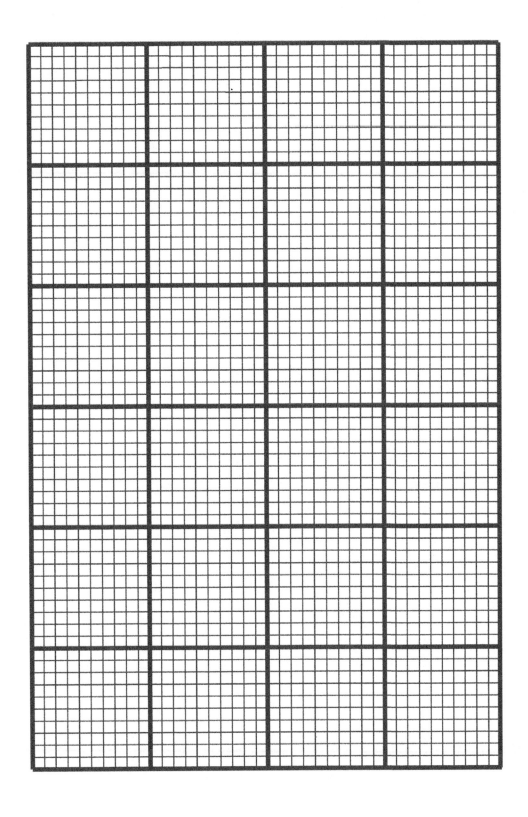

Floss Chart

STRAND	TYPE	NUMBER	COLOR	ALTERNATE

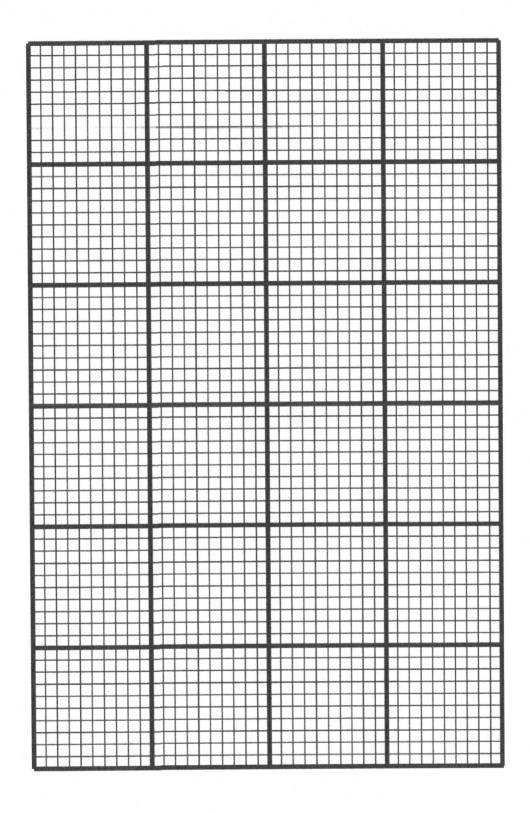

Floss Chart

STRAND	TYPE	NUMBER	COLOR	ALTERNATE

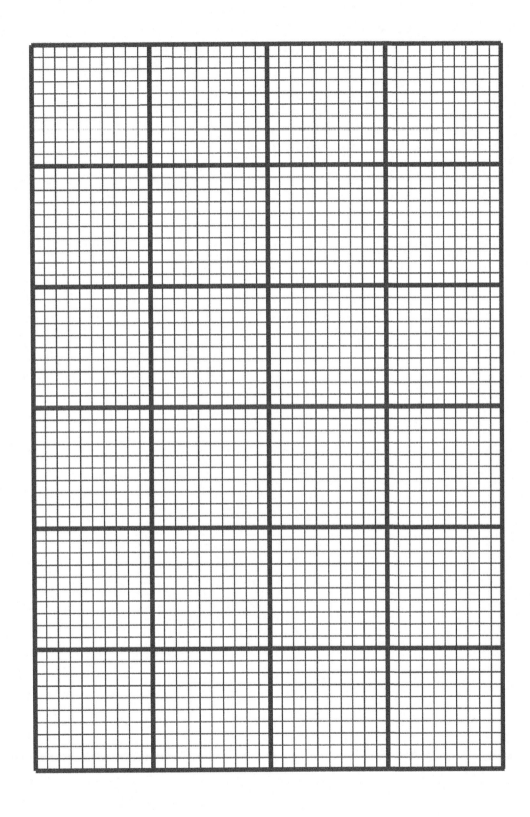

Floss Chart

STRAND	TYPE	NUMBER	COLOR	ALTERNATE

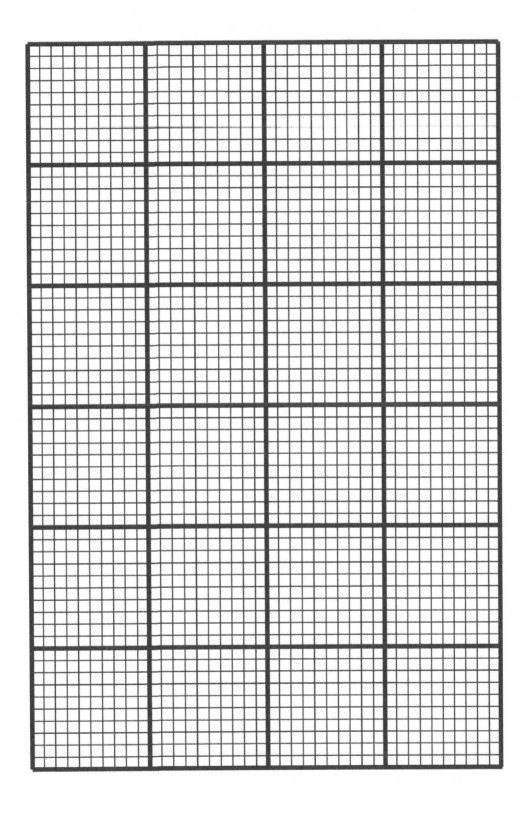

Floss Chart

STRAND	TYPE	NUMBER	COLOR	ALTERNATE

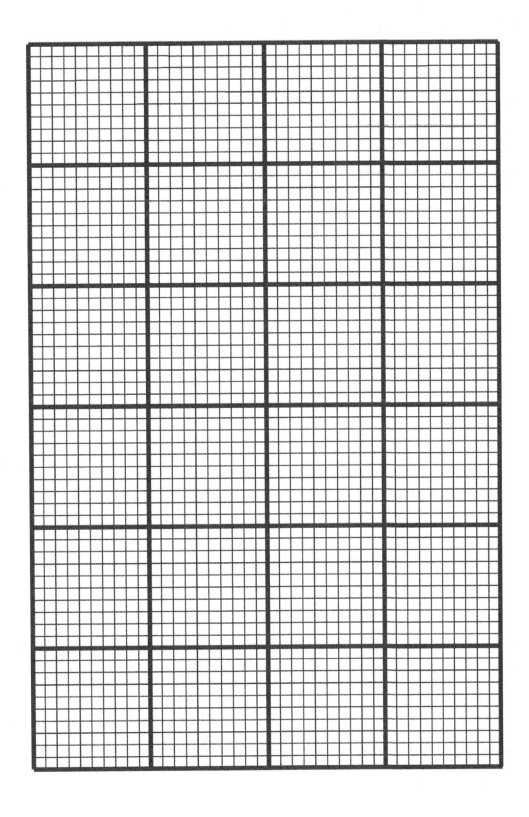

Floss Chart

STRAND	TYPE	NUMBER	COLOR	ALTERNATE

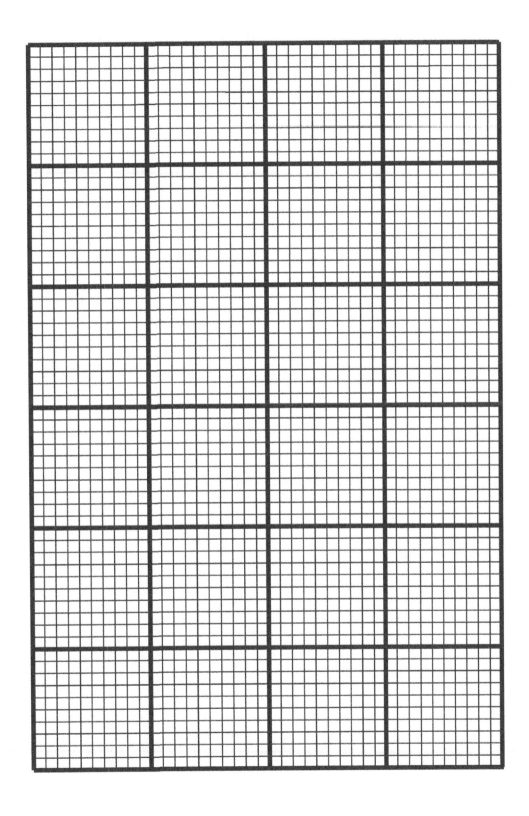

Floss Chart

STRAND	TYPE	NUMBER	COLOR	ALTERNATE

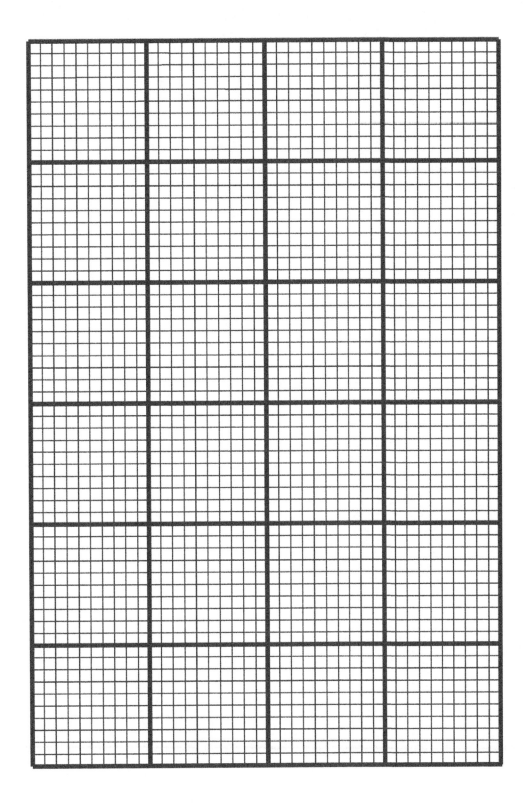

Floss Chart

STRAND	TYPE	NUMBER	COLOR	ALTERNATE

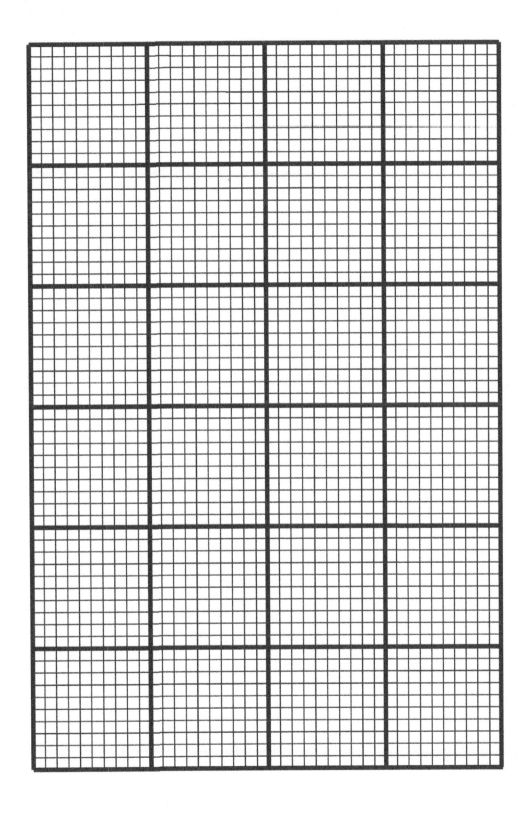

Floss Chart

STRAND	TYPE	NUMBER	COLOR	ALTERNATE

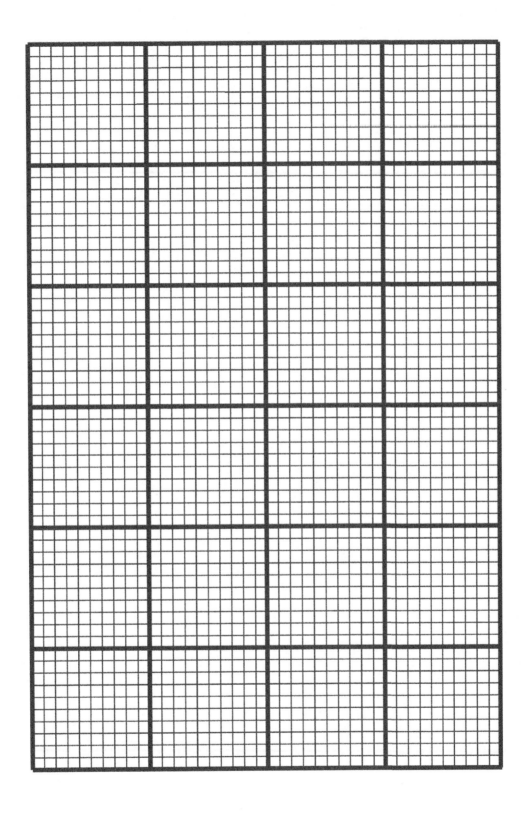

Floss Chart

STRAND	TYPE	NUMBER	COLOR	ALTERNATE

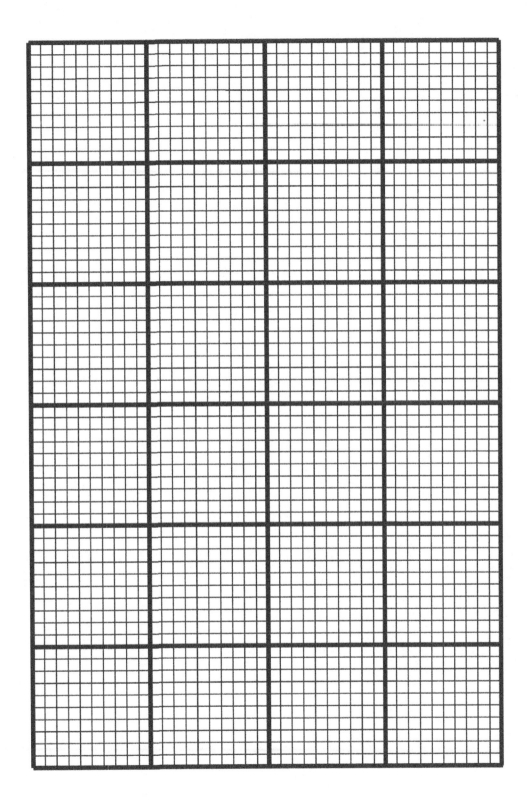

Floss Chart

STRAND	TYPE	NUMBER	COLOR	ALTERNATE

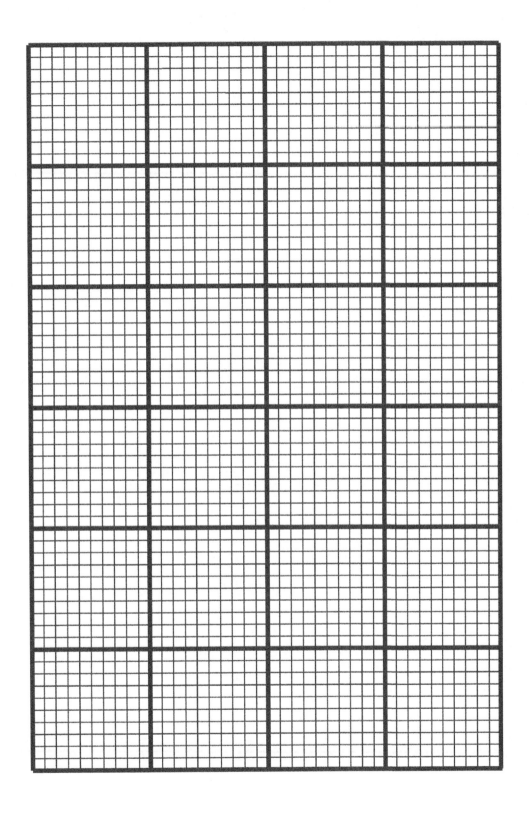

Floss Chart

STRAND	TYPE	NUMBER	COLOR	ALTERNATE

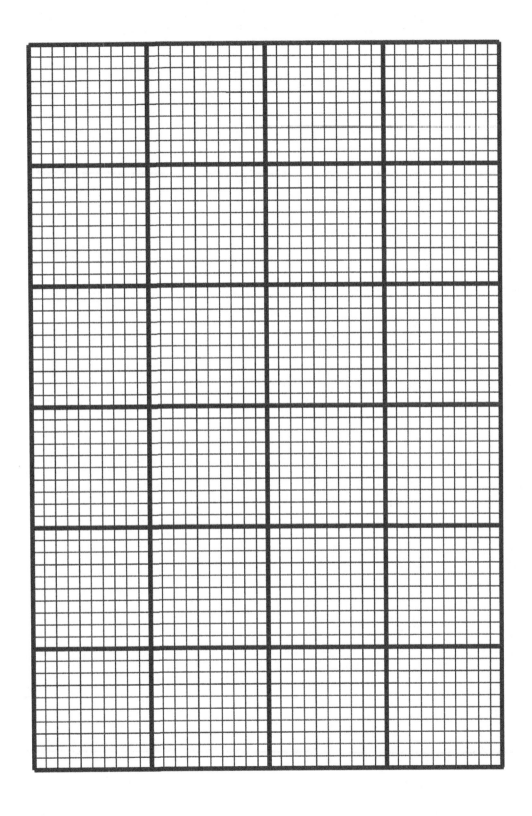

Floss Chart

STRAND	TYPE	NUMBER	COLOR	ALTERNATE

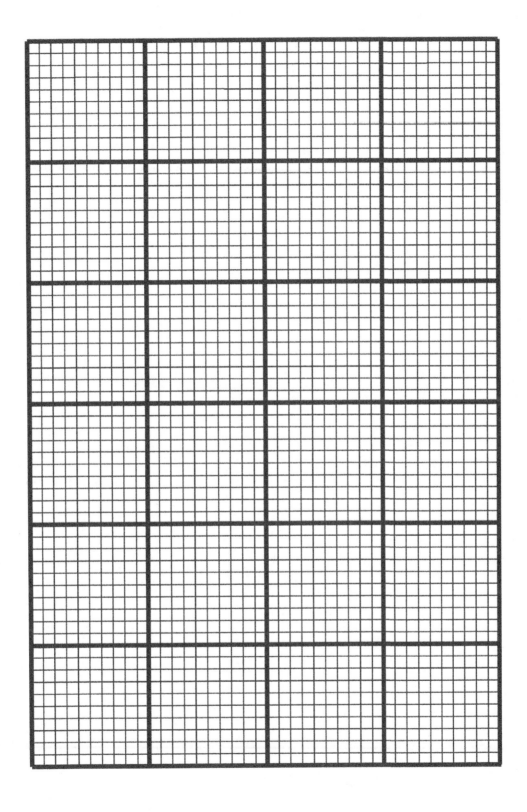

Floss Chart

STRAND	TYPE	NUMBER	COLOR	ALTERNATE

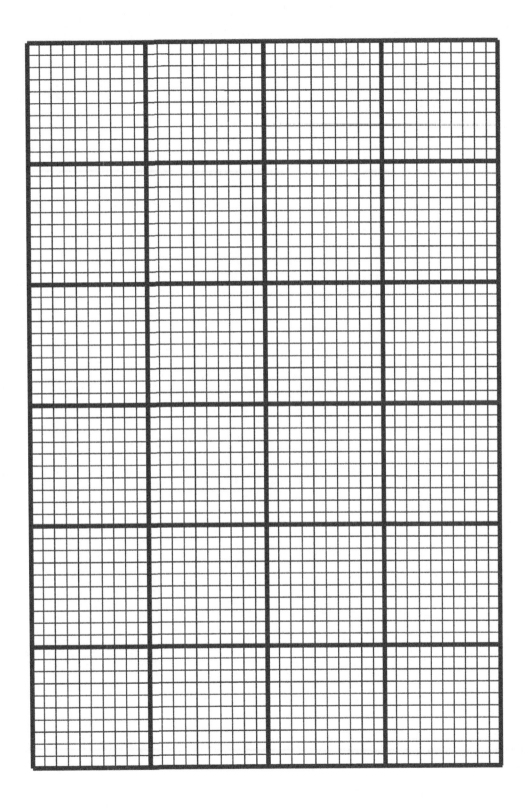

Floss Chart

STRAND	TYPE	NUMBER	COLOR	ALTERNATE

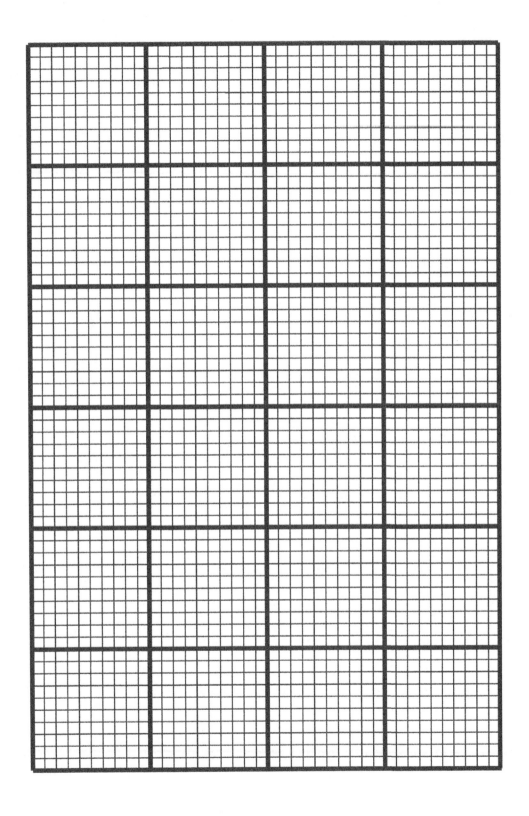

ABOUT HOOP & THREAD NEEDLEWORK DESIGN

Sisters, Arisa Williams and Kim O'Malley
design useful writing journals, diaries, doodle books,
sketch books, list creators and log books for you.

We wish you all the best things in life!

✗ ✗ ✗

Hoop & Thread Needlework Design – Fan-Craft-Tastic Fiber Art Makers Series

Cross Stitch & Needlepoint Chart and Pattern Sketchbook:
Four Sizes of Stitch Count Graphs on 10 Square Grid with Fill In Floss Charts

The Snarky Cross Stabber - DIY Design Supply Journals Series

10-Square Grid Sketchbook for Your Bad*ss Designs:
Draw Your Own Subversive Needlework Charts and Patterns

Brainstorm Journals – Write It Down! Series

Blank Lined Writing Journal

Brainstorm Journals - Love Me, Myself and I Series

Love Letters to Me: A Self Love Blank Lined Journal

1001 Reasons to Love Me: Create Your Own List

Made in the USA
Monee, IL
06 April 2021